'Never mind! Christmas is coming!'

for Sarah

The Victorian Christmas Book

Antony & Peter Miall

Pantheon Books
New York

Library of Congress Cataloging in Publication Data

Miall, Antony
The Victorian Christmas book.

1. Christmas—Great Britain—History.   I. Miall,
Peter, joint author. II. Title.
GT4987.43.M52   1979   394.2′68282′0941   79-1975
ISBN 0-394-50776-2

Manufactured in the United States of America

First American Edition

Acknowledgements.

In any anthology of this kind the editors are always led to a variety of sources
and The Victorian Christmas Book has been no exception. There have been
many sources and many leaders and we cannot name them all. However, we
should like especially to thank the staffs of the London Library and the British
Library, Caroline Goodfellow at the Bethnal Green Museum of Childhood,
Jean Mauldon at the Royal Tunbridge Wells Reference Library, Margaret
Gill and Christopher White at the Royal Tunbridge Wells Museum, Hilary
Kay of Sothebys Belgravia and Jane Langton at the Royal Archives, Windsor
Castle for their invaluable assistance. The section on Christmas cards has been
greatly enhanced by contributions from Harold Cook and Meraud Mason
and for permission to photograph her Christmas plate we are indebted to
Brenda Parsons. We should also like to thank John Goulder for his magnificent
work on the photographs. Above all, though, our thanks are due to Sarah
McCall for her suggestions and contributions to the cookery section as well
as for her occasional criticism and constant encouragement.

In addition, the authors and publishers would like to thank Sothebys
Belgravia for permission to reproduce plates 16–23. Plate 109 is reproduced
by gracious permission of Her Majesty The Queen and colour plates 1, 2, 3,
4, 5 and 9 by permission of the Royal Tunbridge Wells Museum.

Antony Miall and Peter Miall

Contents.

Colour Plates.

6

Introduction.

---◆---

Christmas was gay in the old squire's hall,
Gay at the village inn,
Cheery and loud by the farmer's fire,
Happy the manse within;
But the surest sign of the general joy,
And that all the world was happy—very,
Were the sounds that proved at the workhouse door
That even 'the paupers' were merry.

---◆---

I T MUST have seemed incredible to the Victorians, observing the 'signs of general joy', that anyone had ever disapproved of Christmas. There was, however, a time when Christmas was not only disapproved of, but actually abolished by Act of Parliament. In 1647 under the influence of the Puritans, the observance of the Feast of the Nativity was classed as 'popish' and made a punishable offence. In successive years several priests, congregations and unrepentant revellers were imprisoned for making Christmas Day different to any other. But it was hard to suppress the customs and traditions of 1500 years. Despite the fact that it had been decreed that shops should be kept open and churches closed on 25 December, most Englishmen still kept a small ember of Christmas joy glowing until, with the restoration of the monarchy in 1660, it flared up again into a bonfire. Observance was reinstated and Christmas celebrations became, once more, the order of the day. A contemporary journal—*Poor Robin's Almanack*—expressed popular opinion when it published the following lines:

Now thanks to God for Charles' return
Whose absence made old Christmas mourn;
For then we scarcely did it know,
Whether it Christmas were or no

7

> To feast the poor was counted sin,
> When treason that great praise did win.
> May we ne'er see the like again,
> The roguish Rump should o'er us reign.

But there is no doubt that the 'roguish Rump' had done some damage. Many of the earlier customs and traditions connected with Christmas had been lost and many of them were not to be revived for two hundred years. It was the Victorians with their taste for nostalgia and their keen sense of history who really resurrected Christmas.

Nostalgia for the past and especially for the nineteenth century has been so much in fashion during the last decade that one might be forgiven for thinking it a particularly twentieth-century preoccupation. Few of us think of the Victorians indulging in nostalgia—sentimentality, yes, but nostalgia? In an age in which the march of science became a quickstep, the British 'Red' spread over vast areas of the world map and industrialization grew apace, a feeling for nostalgia is the last thing we would expect to find. And yet, it is there in Victorian art, Victorian music and perhaps above all in the Victorian celebration of Christmas.

Sir Walter Scott looked back longingly at 'Christmas Eve in the Olden Time':

> And well our Christian sires of old
> Loved when the year its course had roll'd,
> And brought blithe Christmas back again,
> With all his hospitable train.
> Domestic and religious rite
> Gave honour to the holy night.

In the next fifty-six lines he went on to describe all aspects of what he understood to be a medieval Christmas—the food, the games and the carols—everything, of course, in the flickering light of the yule log's glow. This idealized picture was certainly very alluring and its appeal to Victorians was very strong indeed. Prompted by their poets and historians, our nineteenth-century ancestors re-created 'old Christmas'. They sanctified it, brought it within the hallowed circle of the hearth, decorated it and imbued it with new customs and such of the old ones as they found acceptable.

As the century went on they added to it. Widening communications produced the Christmas card. Greater prosperity brought the turkey and crackers. A love of home entertainment prompted new 'traditional' Christmas songs and carols, and a love of professional entertainment kept alive the eighteenth-century pantomime and nursed it into rude, rumbustious health. Nostalgia for his homeland led Prince Albert to introduce into England the Christmas tree.

At the heart of all nineteenth-century celebrations of Christmas, however, was the religious significance of the day itself. Middle-class Victorians could not have conceived of Christmas Day without mattins, and from the example they learnt in church they made Christmas a time for giving. Not only did they give presents within the family but also to the less fortunate with whom society abounded. The sounds of joy at the workhouse door were their reward and the exoneration of their own celebrations.

At no time in the year can we see the Victorians being so utterly 'Victorian' as they were at Christmas. Separated into little family knots around the hearth, the table or the piano, they all strove to make their home lives as like as possible to that of their own dear Queen. And she, wife and mother, in the bosom of her family, gave them a perfect example. The Victorians followed the Royal Family's progress from Christmas Eve to Boxing Day—to church and to the table—and strove to do likewise. And while the families celebrated, Victorian writers and artists described their activities and presented to future generations a picture of the Victorian Christmas as they would have liked it to be seen.

The wealth of this material is indeed overwhelming and the present editors must confess to having been bemused by the amount. It would be impossible, in a book this size, to cover adequately every facet of the nineteenth-century Christmas. Whilst every effort has been made to include a representative collection of contemporary descriptions and drawings, certain aspects have had to be omitted. For these omissions we apologize and can only hope that even with them there will be plenty to intrigue and entertain.

Wherever possible we have allowed the Victorians to speak for themselves in the hope that they will reveal far more about their attitudes and beliefs than any modern sociological study could do. For the same reason we have not included any photographs. The cold eye of the camera is notoriously incapable of shedding light on grey areas, and a good drawing or painting speaks volumes about the attitudes of the artist and his models.

Finally a plea on behalf of nostalgia. Nowadays we see it as a symptom of the sick society, but to the Victorians it was a positive force in their search for a means of self-expression. It was one of the starting points for romanticism and, most important here, the main ingredient of that prodigious social edifice of the nineteenth century—The Victorian Christmas—which we should feel no guilt in enjoying to the full.

Christmas Presents.

---◆---

'Christmas won't be Christmas without any presents,'
grumbled Jo, lying on the rug.

Little Women, LOUISA M. ALCOTT, 1868

---◆---

A S IT turned out, Jo and the other girls received hardly any presents at all. But giving presents has always been as much fun as getting them, and so Miss Alcott's heroines saved all their pocket money and spent it on gifts for Marmee—a pair of slippers, some handkerchiefs, a pair of gloves and a large bottle of cologne. And if the giving was fun, then the shopping was even more so. Christmas shopping in nineteenth-century America was as hectic and exciting as it was in England. Howard Paul describes the scene in 'Christmas in America', 1885:

> The presentation of 'boxes' and souvenirs is the same in America as in England ... everybody expects to give and receive. A month before the event the fancy stores are crowded all day long with old and young in search of suitable souvenirs, and every object is purchased, from the costliest gems to the tawdriest babiole that may get into the market. If the weather should be fine, the principal streets are thronged with ladies shopping in sleighs: and hither and thither sleds shoot by, laden with parcels of painted toys, instruments of mock music and septuagenarian dread, from a penny trumpet to a sheepskin drum.

While in London, gaily-decorated shop fronts added to the mood of anticipation. George R. Sims paints this picture:

> A mighty magician has touched London with his wand. The spirit of altruism has descended upon the city of self. The note of preparation for the great festival of the Christian Church, which was sounded early in November when the windows of the stationers, the booksellers' shops, and the railway stalls

11

1 Christmas shopping in the Lowther Arcade. The children's faces are alight with excitement as they point to all the gifts, especially the dolls, hanging from the sides of the narrow thoroughfare (1870).

2 A satisfactory shopping expedition. A well-to-do mother and her daughter leave the store, and a footman follows with the chosen family presents (c. 1890).

3 'Oh! we've all been shopping, shop, shop, shopping, we've visited the Lowther and
the Burlington Arcade
And we're all of us a-dropping, drop, drop, dropping fast asleep, except Papa, that
idle man, who only paid.' (1876)

became suddenly gay with the coloured plates of Christmas numbers innumerable, has increased in volume as time went on. Now, on the eve of the great day, there is not a street in the capital containing a shop, from its broadest thoroughfare to its narrowest by-way, that has not decked its windows for the Christmas market.

If the potential purchaser could not come to the shop, then the shop would come to the purchaser through the medium of its own catalogues or through lavish advertisements in the December numbers of popular magazines, fully illustrated and complete with winning, seductive copy. In *The Ladies' Field* of December 1898 the following appeared:

Our illustrations will furnish some idea of the charms of the Yuletide gifts at Messrs Dickins and Jones's, and further must be noted the charming assortment of 'Olympia' glass, and the blue and white Dresden ware. Of the latter the candlesticks are particularly desirable, and there are some charmingly shaped dishes which might equally well be adopted for use or ornamenta-

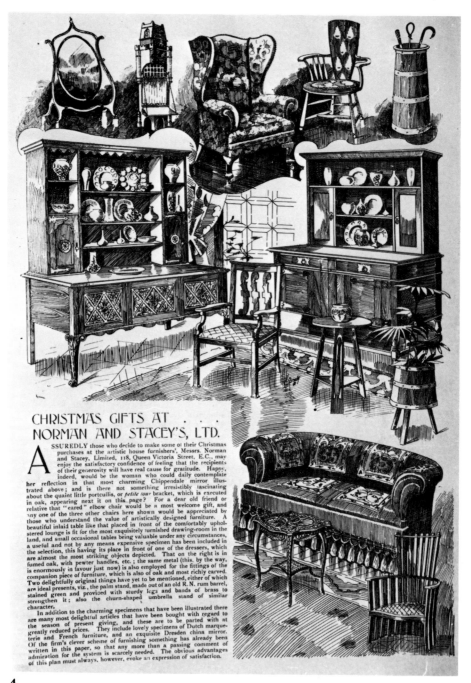

CHRISTMAS GIFTS AT . . .
NORMAN AND STACEY'S, LTD.

ASSUREDLY those who decide to make some of their Christmas purchases at the artistic house furnishers', Messrs. Norman and Stacey, Limited, 118, Queen Victoria Street, E.C., may enjoy the satisfactory confidence of feeling that the recipients of their generosity will have real cause for gratitude. Happy, indeed, would be the woman who could daily contemplate her reflection in that most charming Chippendale mirror illustrated above; and is there not something irresistibly fascinating about the quaint little portcullis, or *petite tour* bracket, which is executed in oak, appearing next it on this page? For a dear old friend or relative that "eared" elbow chair would be a most welcome gift, and any one of the three other chairs here shown would be appreciated by those who understand the value of artistically designed furniture. A beautiful inlaid table like that placed in front of the comfortably upholstered lounge is fit for the most exquisitely furnished drawing-room in the land, and small occasional tables being valuable under any circumstances, a useful and not by any means expensive specimen has been included in the selection, this having its place in front of one of the dressers, which are almost the most striking objects depicted. That on the right is in fumed oak, with pewter handles, etc.; the same metal (this, by the way, is enormously in favour just now) is also employed for the fittings of the companion piece of furniture, which is also of oak and most richly carved. Two delightfully original things have yet to be mentioned, either of which are ideal presents, viz., the palm stand, made out of an old R.N. rum barrel, stained green and provided with sturdy legs and bands of brass to strengthen it; also the churn-shaped umbrella stand of similar character.

In addition to the charming specimens that have been illustrated there are many most delightful articles that have been bought with regard to the season of present giving, and these are to be parted with at greatly reduced prices. They include lovely specimens of Dutch marqueterie and French furniture, and an exquisite Dresden china mirror. Of the firm's clever scheme of furnishing something has already been written in this paper, so that any more than a passing comment of admiration for the system is scarcely needed. The obvious advantages of this plan must always, however, evoke an expression of satisfaction.

4

IN SEARCH
OF A CHRISTMAS PRESENT.

IT is pleasant to remember that, in these days of change and upheaval, the good old custom of indicating one's friendship and esteem by a present, more or less costly, beautiful, or useful, survives.

Indeed, these kindly interchanges form no small part of the enjoyment of the festive season. While on

the continent and across the border New Year's Day is the selected date, yet the Britisher, whether at home or in distant colony, clings to Christmastide as the most befitting time. The custom is a pleasant one, blessing those who give as well as those that receive; but it is by no means an easy task to select a suitable present. So many points have to be considered— what will be acceptable, what its cost, and, above all, where to buy, are important considerations. Our readers, especially those resident in the country, whose time when in London is comparatively limited, and who wish to save the fatigue and worry of journeying from shop to shop, may be glad of a few suggestive hints as to where to seek and what to buy for a Christmas or New Year's present.

It will be assumed that something useful is desired— not something that is practically a white elephant, nor an article of exceptional cost—and in that case there is probably no place where there is a wider range of choice than at Maple's, in Tottenham Court Road. Maple's may be regarded as a perennial Exhibition. Other Exhibitions come and go, but Maple remains, and the

visitor need never fear that he or she will see there only the stereotyped or commonplace articles found in any ordinary shop. An Exhibition it is indeed, the floor space covering many acres, and something new, fresh, and artistic always to be seen. Sketch 1, for example, is a Turkish lounge, which is most delightful in its conception—its wide, roomy settee, in saddlebags and velvet upholstered in a manner luxurious enough to

captivate the heart of the great Caliph Haroun Alraschid, while the embroidered drapery of the doorway is quite unique in its quaintness and beauty. Comfortable

lounges, settees, and really easy chairs are a speciality of Maple's, and as such things are made in their own factories, they are able to do much better for their patrons than the Stores, or other firms who have to buy from the actual makers. We recently saw a Haddon easy-chair, covered in tapestry and trimmed with fringe, that had been supplied at something less than fifty shillings, a perfect marvel of cheapness.

Screens are always regarded as suitable presents. A screen is ever useful. It prevents draughts. It secures privacy. Who does not appreciate a cup of tea and a friendly chat, protected from the busybody or the tattler by the friendly screen? Maple's have a lovely choice of screens for this year, including some admirable specimens in Louis XV. and Japanese panellings.

Cosy Corners are decidedly English in their origin and conception, and their early prototypes may be seen in many an olden gabled and mullioned mansion.

The idea is good, though it is a mistake to put a cheap, slightly made thing of this kind into an otherwise well-furnished room. Cosy Corners should be substantially made, and those at Maple's seem all that can be desired.

But while it is delightful and interesting to write of Cosy Corners and Turkish Lounges, yet it is scarcely in this direction, perhaps, that Christmas presents will be sought, and it may therefore be helpful to refer to other departments. For example, several saloons are devoted to useful articles of furniture, the cost of which may be covered by five pounds—for instance, delightfully soft and inviting easy-chairs, bureaux, writing-tables, easels, pedestals, card-tables, music-cabinets, tea and coffee tables, escritoires, gossip-chairs, cabinets, small bookcases, and other articles too numerous to attempt to describe; while for more important presents there are library chairs in morocco, tables, Wooton and Grosvenor cabinets, smoking-chairs, and other objects. A little book, with nearly 400 illustrations, is posted gratis.

Among the elegant cabinets exhibited, a very fine one in Japanese style (sketch 2) greatly took our fancy, as did also some other examples, which we readily recognised as reproductions from the ancient French palaces at Versailles, the Louvre, and the Grand Trianon.

The floor lamps, one of which is illustrated in sketch 4, are in greater demand than ever, and cannot fail to be acceptable as a present for either the manor-house drawing-room or the cosy study at the rectory. The favourite metals are polished brass and copper, or hammered iron with brass or copper relief-work. A very nice specimen can be had for a couple of pounds, or even less, and Maple's have issued a new illustrated price-list of these goods for the guidance of their country customers. Every lamp is fitted with a patent self-extinguishing burner, thus ensuring absolute safety. Many of the new shades are simply lovely.

The show-rooms for clocks, bronzes, and porcelain vases are always attractive. Sketch 5 represents a very charming mercury gilt Louis XV. clock, while we were delighted with another specimen, also in mercury gilt, being a facsimile of one in the Marie Antoinette room at Fontainebleau.

The delicately beautiful Crown Derby and Coalport china quite won our admiration, as did the Boon ware. This latter has very gracefully delineated floral decorations, mostly on dull ivory grounds, though some other pieces were gold clouded, resembling Satsuma ware, and, to our surprise, the prices for really handsome pieces ranged from only six or seven shillings up to a couple of guineas. Sketch 3 illustrates some of the shapes.

Passing through show-rooms full of tempting Eastern embroideries and lovely silken and other curtain textures, and catching a glimpse of a series of great rooms, where piles upon piles of rare Indian and Persian carpets and prayer-rugs are shown, we came to a vast area devoted to wicker chairs in every variety of shape and drapery, quaint cabinets, tables and stands in bamboo with lacquer trays. A chair with long roomy seat, the "Egyptian," struck us as being the acme of comfort.

The new show-rooms for sterling silver and electro-plate next claimed our attention. This section of Maple's warehouse is always a favourite resort of those in search of wedding and christening gifts, as well as Christmas presents, and the firm now prominently exhibit Louis Quinze and Empire designs in both silver and silver plate, with the old dull unburnished finish. A charming example of a Louis XV. mirror and candelabra are illustrated in sketch 6.

In other well-appointed show-rooms were dining-room, drawing-room, and bed-room furniture in every

conceivable variety of style, while from adjacent great buildings we heard the whirr and rush of machinery, and saw in large well-lighted factories hosts of workers, busily engaged in the various branches of production.

Asking, as a matter of curiosity, how many persons were employed in this colossal Tottenham Court Road establishment, with all its appurtenances, we learned that the number was nearly 3000, exclusive of those who work indirectly or occasionally.

Mechanical Marvels at Swears & Wells's.

MUSICAL MECHANICAL DOLL.

MUSICAL DANCING CAT.

A VERY charming little comedy is being enacted daily in the toy department at Swears and Wells's, 190 and 192, Regent Street, W. True, the actors will only perform their parts on one condition, and that is that you will turn the key of the musical-box which represents their mimic stage, but once you have performed this office they are quite independent henceforth of your services.

One of the two figures in the centre group on this page is a dainty little French *bonne* who is knitting quietly on the double bench, just as many another *bonne* has sat knitting before now in the Bois de Boulogne, and the other is a dashing French soldier.

Fast as the *bonne's* little fingers fly—and she is never idle—the stocking at which she is working so assiduously never grows longer, for, hard as it is to believe, this demure little person, in her tucked silk shirt and neat white apron, and her gallant com-

panion, are nothing more than mechanical toys.

But what wonderful things these toys can do! Heads, hands, lips, limbs, and eyes move in faithful imitation of those expressive little gestures by which the French manage to convey infinitely more meaning than by mere words; and it is easy enough for the youngest child to follow the drift of the dumb show that is being carried on. Every movement that the poor little soldier makes shows how terribly *épris* he is with his charming companion, and how earnestly he begs and entreats of her to take his flowers, and how charmingly she shakes her head, glancing up at him ever and anon coquettishly from under her eyelashes, never relaxing her knitting, and finally putting a climax to the affair by turning her back upon him.

Human beings could not do it more naturally or spontaneously than do these wonderful dolls.

But there are other waxen people at 190 and 192, Regent Street who are quite as clever and wide awake as the French *bonne* and her soldier. There is the banjo player—dressed in his gorgeous brocade coat and orthodox striped

FRENCH SOLDIER AND MAID.

silk shirt, and please notice his neat little leather boots and socks —who twangs his banjo, winks his eyes, and shrugs his shoulders in time to his music, his mouth moving as though, in very sooth, the words were issuing from his lips, while the air played by the musical-box conveys the distinct sound of a voice singing.

Notice, too, the gentleman in bright blue silk tail coat, with large gilt buttons, grey beaver hat, and huge variegated tie, trolling out a light-hearted song, the while he shares his bread with his sociable companion, the pig, who is quite willing to refresh himself with a mouthful whenever it is handed to him.

But, remarkable as all this was, I was still more amazed to hear (considering the time of year) the sound of a bird singing. Such a beautiful song, too—you might easily have taken it for that of a nightingale, if you can imagine a nightingale in December; and the little songster, in his gilded cage, was opening and shutting his beak to let the melody out in rippling runs and trills, and dancing on his perch, as though there was no rain or gloom outside to quench his ardour.

And yet this bird, like the *bonne*, the banjo player, or the French soldier, requires no food, drink, or sleep to keep him going, and owes his song to the little brass key cunningly hidden away at the back of the cage.

I could tell you of a great many more curious things at Messrs. Swears and Wells's. There are the toy children, who, in their turn, enjoy a good game with diminutive toys of their own, as, for instance, the little maid in the pink silk frock in our illustration, who is amusing herself immensely with a donkey, which she draws by a string, and a beautiful dollie in white satin, all the figures moving as prettily and naturally as in real life. And there is the white cat, a very smart person indeed, with his silver-topped cane and beautiful bouquet, who waltzes as smoothly and gracefully as though he had just perfected his education at a dancing academy; while the skin elephant on wheels, who trumpets in the most

natural manner possible, may be counted a worthy rival to our favourite at the Zoo, for he is quite as ready to take the children for endless rides in the comfortable little leather seat on his back. Nearly all the animals in fact, at 190 and 192, Regent Street can talk in their own particular language, even if they cannot perform some wonderful feat or other that would make the old-fashioned toys our mothers and grandmothers were content to play with green with envy.

Be sure, too, to look at the model stables and the soldiers, for of both there is a grand supply for the children's Christmas gifts. And last, but not least, when you pay your visit to this children's paradise, as assuredly you will, do not forget to ask to see the bazaar game, where the mechanical clown runs up the pole and brings down one of the toys, all of which are numbered. This is a capital amusement for a children's party, as each child chooses a number, and the excitement of seeing which article the clever little climber will catch first as they spin round makes the fun fast and furious.

THE SOCIABLE PIG.

NIGGER BANJO PLAYER.

Victorian magazines carried many articles and features before Christmas dispensing advice and information about buying presents. The 'artistic house furnishers', Messrs Norman and Stacey Ltd, wish their customers to note their palm stand and umbrella stand, made from old Royal Navy rum barrels (**4**), Maples in Tottenham Court Road is a 'perennial exhibition' (**5**), and Swears and Wells have 'mechanical marvels' including musical toys ranging from a dancing cat to a 'sociable pig' (**6**).

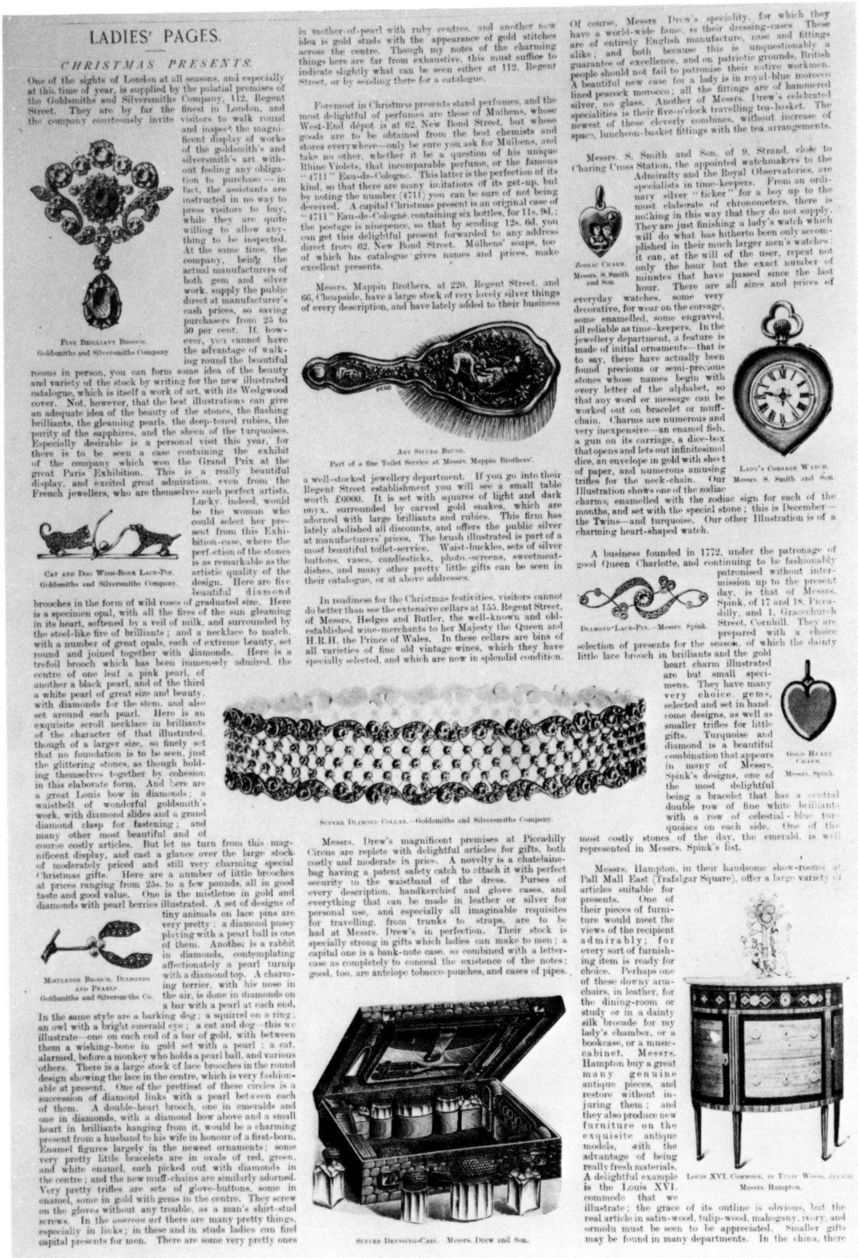

LADIES' PAGES.

CHRISTMAS PRESENTS.

One of the sights of London at all seasons, and especially at this time of year, is supplied by the palatial premises of the Goldsmiths and Silversmiths Company, 112, Regent Street. They are by far the finest in London, and the company courteously invite visitors to walk round and inspect the magnificent display of works of the goldsmith's and silversmith's art without feeling any obligation to purchase — in fact, the assistants are instructed in no way to press visitors to buy, while they are quite willing to allow anything to be inspected. At the same time, the company, being the actual manufacturers of both gem and silver work, supply the public direct at manufacturer's cash prices, so saving purchasers from 25 to 50 per cent. If, however, you cannot have the advantage of walking round the beautiful rooms in person, you can form some idea of the beauty and variety of the stock by writing for the new illustrated catalogue, which is itself a work of art, with its Wedgwood cover. Not, however, that the best illustrations can give an adequate idea of the beauty of the stones, the flashing brilliants, the gleaming pearls, the deep-toned rubies, the purity of the sapphires, and the sheen of the turquoises. Especially desirable is a personal visit this year, for there is to be seen a case containing the exhibit of the company which won the Grand Prix at the great Paris Exhibition. This is a truly beautiful display, and excited great admiration, even from the French jewellers, who are themselves such perfect artists.

Fine Brilliant Brooch. Goldsmiths and Silversmiths Company.

Lucky, indeed, would be the woman who could select her present from this Exhibition-case, where the perfection of the stones is as remarkable as the artistic quality of the design. Here are five beautiful diamond brooches in the form of wild roses of graduated size. Here is a specimen opal, with all the fires of the sun gleaming in its heart, softened by a veil of milk, and surrounded by the steel-like fire of brilliants; and a necklace to match, with a number of great opals, each of extreme beauty, set round and joined together with diamonds. Here is a trefoil brooch which has been immensely admired, the centre of one leaf a pink pearl, of another a black pearl, and of the third a white pearl of great size and beauty, with diamonds for the stem, and also set around each pearl. Here is an exquisite scroll necklace in brilliants of the character of that illustrated, though of a larger size, so finely set that no foundation is to be seen, just the glittering stones, as though holding themselves together by cohesion in this elaborate form. And here are a great Louis bow in diamonds, a waistbelt of wonderful goldsmith's work, with diamond slides and a grand diamond clasp for fastening; and many other most beautiful and of course costly articles. But let us turn from this magnificent display, and cast a glance over the large stock of moderately priced and still very charming special Christmas gifts.

Cat and Dog Wine-Book Lock-Pin. Goldsmiths and Silversmiths Company.

Here are a number of little brooches at prices ranging from 25s. to a few pounds, all in good taste and good value. One is the mistletoe in gold and diamonds with pearl berries illustrated. A set of designs of tiny animals or lace pins are very pretty; a diamond pussy playing with a pearl ball is one of them. Another is a rabbit in diamonds, contemplating affectionately a pearl turnip with a diamond top. A charming terrier, with his nose in the air, is there in diamonds on a bar with a pearl at each end.

Mistletoe Brooch, Diamonds and Pearls. Goldsmiths and Silversmiths Co.

In the same style are a barking dog; a squirrel on a ring; an owl with a bright emerald eye; a cat and dog — this we illustrate — one on each end of a bar of gold, with between them a wishing-bone in gold set with a pearl; a cat, alarmed, before a monkey who holds a pearl ball, and various others. There is a large stock of lace brooches in the round design showing the lace in the centre, which is very fashionable at present. One of the prettiest of these circles is a succession of diamond links with a pearl between each of them. A double-heart brooch, one in emeralds and one in diamonds, with a diamond bow above and a small heart in brilliants hanging from it, would be a charming present from a husband to his wife in honour of a first-born. Enamel figures largely in the newest ornaments; some very pretty little bracelets are in ovals of red, green, and white enamel, each picked out with diamonds in the centre; and the new muff-chains are similarly adorned. Very pretty trifles are sets of glove-buttons, some in enamel, some in gold with gems in the centre. They screw on the gloves without any trouble, as a man's shirt-stud screws. In the same way there are many pretty things, especially in links; in these and in studs ladies can find capital presents for men. There are some very pretty ones

in mother-of-pearl with ruby centres, and another new idea is gold studs with the appearance of gold stitches across the centre. Though my notes of the charming things here are far from exhaustive, this must suffice to indicate slightly what can be seen either at 112, Regent Street, or by sending there for a catalogue.

Foremost in Christmas presents stand perfumes, and the most delightful of perfumes are those of Mülhens, the West-End dépôt is at 62, New Bond Street, but whose goods are to be obtained from the best chemists and stores everywhere — only be sure you ask for Mülhens, and take no other, whether it be a question of his unique Rhine Violets, that incomparable perfume, or the famous "4711" Eau-de-Cologne. This latter is the perfection of its kind, so that there are many imitations of its get-up, but by noting the number (4711) you can be sure of not being deceived. A capital Christmas present is an original case of "4711" Eau-de-Cologne, containing six bottles, for 11s. 9d.; the postage is ninepence, so that by sending 12s. 6d. you can get this delightful present forwarded to any address direct from 62, New Bond Street. Mülhens' soaps, too, of which his catalogue gives names and prices, make excellent presents.

Messrs. Mappin Brothers, at 220, Regent Street, and 66, Cheapside, have a large stock of very lovely silver things of every description, and have lately added to their business

Art Silver Brush. Part of a fine Toilet Service at Messrs. Mappin Brothers.

a well-stocked jewellery department. If you go into their Regent Street establishment you will see a small table worth £6000. It is set with squares of light and dark onyx, surrounded by carved gold snakes, which are adorned with large brilliants and rubies. This firm has lately abolished all discounts, and offers the public silver at manufacturers' prices. The brush illustrated is part of a most beautiful toilet-service. Waist-buckles, sets of silver buttons, vases, candlesticks, photo.-screens, sweetmeat-dishes, and many other pretty little gifts can be seen in their catalogue, or at above addresses.

In readiness for the Christmas festivities, visitors cannot do better than see the extensive cellars at 155, Regent Street, of Messrs. Hedges and Butler, the well-known and old-established wine-merchants to her Majesty the Queen and H.R.H. the Prince of Wales. In these cellars are bins of all varieties of fine old vintage wines, which they have specially selected, and which are now in splendid condition.

Silver Diamond Collar. Goldsmiths and Silversmiths Company.

Messrs. Drew's magnificent premises at Piccadilly Circus are replete with delightful articles for gifts, both costly and moderate in price. A novelty is a combination-bag having a patent safety catch to attach it with perfect security to the waistband of the dress. Purses of every description, handkerchief and glove cases, and everything that can be made in leather or silver for personal use, and especially all imaginable requisites for travelling, from trunks to straps, are to be had at Messrs. Drew's in perfection. Their stock is specially strong in gifts which ladies can make to men; a capital one is a bank-note case, so combined with a letter-case as completely to conceal the existence of the notes; good, too, are antelope tobacco-pouches, and cases of pipes.

Silver Dressing-Case. Messrs. Drew and Son.

Of course, Messrs. Drew's speciality, for which they have a world-wide fame, is their dressing-cases. These are of entirely English manufacture, case and fittings alike; and both because this is unquestionably a guarantee of excellence, and on patriotic grounds, British people should not fail to patronise their native workmen. A beautiful new case for a lady is in royal-blue morocco lined peacock morocco, all the fittings are of hammered silver, no glass. Another of Messrs. Drew's celebrated specialities is their five-o'clock travelling tea-basket. The newest of these cleverly combines, without increase of space, luncheon-basket fittings with the tea arrangements.

Messrs. S. Smith and Son, of 9, Strand, close to Charing Cross Station, the appointed watchmakers to the Admiralty and the Royal Observatories, are specialists in time-keepers. From an ordinary silver "ticker" for a boy up to the

Zodiac Charm. Messrs. S. Smith and Son.

most elaborate of chronometers, there is nothing in this way that they do not supply. They are just finishing a lady's watch which will do what has hitherto been only accomplished in their much larger men's watches — it can, at the will of the user, repeat not only the hour but the exact number of minutes that have passed since the last hour. There are all sizes and prices of everyday watches, some very decorative, for wear on the corsage; some enamelled, some engraved, all reliable as time-keepers. In the jewellery department, a feature is made of initial ornaments — that is to say, there have actually been found precious or semi-precious stones whose names begin with every letter of the alphabet, so that any word or message can be worked out on bracelet or muff-chain. Charms are numerous and very inexpensive — an enamel fish, a gun on its carriage, a dice-box that opens and lets out infinitesimal dice, an envelope in gold with sheet of paper, and numerous amusing trifles for the neck-chain. Our Illustration shows one of the zodiac charms; enamelled with the zodiac sign for each of the months, and set with the special stone; this is December — the Twins — and turquoise. Our other Illustration is of a charming heart-shaped watch.

Lady's Corsage Watch. Messrs. S. Smith and Son.

A business founded in 1772, under the patronage of good Queen Charlotte, and continuing to be fashionably patronised without intermission up to the present day, is that of Messrs. Spink, of 17 and 18, Piccadilly, and 1, Gracechurch Street, Cornhill. They are prepared with a choice selection of presents for the season, of which the dainty little lace brooch in brilliants and the gold heart charm illustrated are but small specimens. They have many very choice gems, selected and set in handsome designs, as well as smaller trifles for little gifts. Turquoise and diamond is a favourite combination that appears in many of Messrs. Spink's designs, one of the most delightful being a bracelet that has a central double row of fine white brilliants with a row of celestial-blue turquoises on each side. One of the most costly stones of the day, the emerald, is well represented in Messrs. Spink's list.

Diamond Lace-Pin. Messrs. Spink.

Gold Heart Charm.

Messrs. Hampton, in their handsome show-rooms at Pall Mall East (Trafalgar Square), offer a large variety of articles suitable for presents. One of their pieces of furniture would meet the views of the recipient admirably; for every sort of furnishing item is ready for choice. Perhaps one of these downy arm-chairs, in leather, for the dining-room or study or in a dainty silk brocade for my lady's chamber, or a bookcase, or a music-cabinet. Messrs. Hampton buy a great many genuine antique pieces, and restore without injuring them; and they also produce new furniture on the exquisite antique models, with the advantage of being really fresh materials. A delightful example is the Louis XVI. commode that we illustrate; the grace of its outline is obvious, but the real article in satin-wood, mahogany, ivory, and ormolu must be seen to be appreciated. Smaller gifts may be found in many departments. In the china, there

Louis XVI. Commode, in Tulip Wood, Inlaid. Messrs. Hampton.

7 Christmas present vignettes from the 'Ladies Pages' of the *Illustrated London News* of 1900.

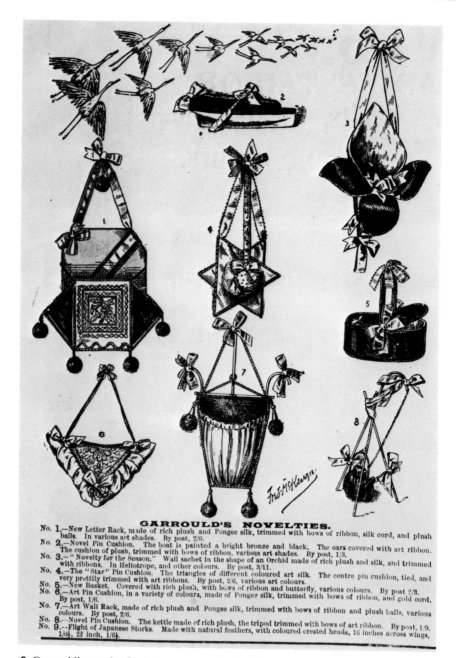

GARROULD'S NOVELTIES.

No. 1.—New Letter Rack, made of rich plush and Pongee silk, trimmed with bows of ribbon, silk cord, and plush balls. In various art shades. By post, 2/6.

No. 2.—Novel Pin Cushion. The boat is painted a bright bronze and black. The oars covered with art ribbon. The cushion of plush, trimmed with bows of ribbon, various art shades. By post, 1/3.

No. 3.—"Novelty for the Season." Wall sachet in the shape of an Orchid made of rich plush and silk, and trimmed with ribbons. In Heliotrope, and other colours. By post, 3/11.

No. 4.—The "Star" Pin Cushion. The triangles of different coloured art silk. The centre pin cushion, tied, and very prettily trimmed with art ribbons. By post, 2/6, various art colours.

No. 5.—New Basket. Covered with rich plush, with bows of ribbon and butterfly, various colours. By post 2/3.

No. 6.—Art Pin Cushion, in a variety of colours, made of Pongee silk, trimmed with bows of ribbon, and gold cord. By post, 1/6.

No. 7.—Art Wall Rack, made of rich plush and Pongee silk, trimmed with bows of ribbon and plush balls, various colours. By post, 2/6.

No. 8.—Novel Pin Cushion. The kettle made of rich plush, the tripod trimmed with bows of art ribbon. By post, 1/9.

No. 9.—Flight of Japanese Storks. Made with natural feathers, with coloured crested heads, 16 inches across wings, 1/0½, 22 inch, 1/6½.

8 Garrould's novelty Christmas presents in the 1890s. Most of them seen to have been varieties of pin cushions.

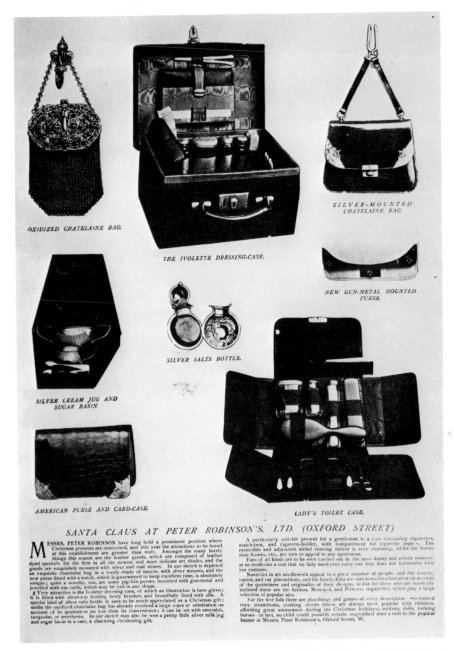

OXIDIZED CHATELAINE BAG.

THE IVOLETTE DRESSING-CASE.

SILVER-MOUNTED
CHATELAINE BAG.

NEW GUN-METAL MOUNTED
PURSE.

SILVER CREAM JUG AND
SUGAR BASIN.

SILVER SALTS BOTTLE.

AMERICAN PURSE AND CARD-CASE.

LADY'S TOILET CASE.

SANTA CLAUS AT PETER ROBINSON'S, LTD. (OXFORD STREET)

MESSRS. PETER ROBINSON have long held a prominent position where Christmas presents are concerned, and this year the attractions to be found at this establishment are greater than ever. Amongst the many lovely things this season are the leather goods, which are composed of leather dyed specially for the firm in all the newest and most delicate art shades, and the goods are exquisitely mounted with silver and real stones. In our sketch is depicted an exquisite chatelaine bag in a lovely shade of mauve, with silver mounts, and the new purse fitted with a watch, which is guaranteed to keep excellent time, is absolutely unique; quite a novelty, too, are some pig-skin purses, mounted with gun-metal and jewelled with em-ralds, which may be had in any shape.

Very attractive is the Ivolette dressing case, of which an illustration is here given; it is fitted with silver-top bottles, ivory brushes, and beautifully lined with silk. A special kind of silver salts bottle is sure to be much appreciated as a Christmas gift; whilst the oxidized chatelaine bag has already received a large share of admiration on account of its quaintness no less than its convenience; it can be set with emeralds, turquoise, or amethysts. In our sketch may also be seen a pretty little silver milk jug and sugar ba in in a case, a charming christening gift.

A particularly suitable present for a gentleman is a case containing cigarettes, match-box, and cigarette-holder, with compartment for cigarette pape s. The reversible and adjustable nickel shaving mirror is very charming, whilst the horse-shoe frames, etc., are sure to appeal to any sportsman.

Fans of all kinds are to be seen carried out in the most dainty and artistic manner, at so moderate a cost that no lady need ever carry one that does not harmonise with her costume.

Novelties in art needlework appeal to a great number of people, and the rosette, carrot, and cat pincushions, and the handy Zulu are sure to excite admiration on account of the quaintness and originality of their designs, whilst for those who are musically inclined there are the Ariston, Monopol, and Princess organettes, which play a large selection of popular airs.

For the wee folk there are playthings and games of every description—mechanical toys, steamboats, cooking stoves (these are always most popular with children, affording great amusement during the Christmas holidays), soldiers, dolls, rocking horses—in fact, no child could possibly remain ungratified after a visit to the popular bazaar at Messrs. Peter Robinson's, Oxford Street, W.

9 A page from the Christmas catalogue of Peter Robinson Ltd, the famous Oxford Street store. Leather goods, apparently, were the star feature of the year.

tion. In fact, so numerous are the gifts at Hannover House, that it would be far too colossal a task to chronicle their merits at length; far better is it to advise our readers to make a personal inspection without delay, or where distance does not admit of this, Messrs Dickins and Jones's catalogue of Christmas presents should be at once sent for. We can answer for it that the only difficulty will be to limit one's purchases, so fascinating are all the goods illustrated therein.

If 'blue and white Dresden ware' or 'Olympia glass' should have proved too expensive for the Victorian Christmas present-giver, then he or she could find any number of magazine articles giving instructions on how to make 'the most perfect of Christmas gifts' at home. From chocolates to chess-boards, from paintings to patchwork, all that were needed, the articles assured, were patience and application. And when, say, the velvet-covered commonplace book with the satin-embroidered bookmarker was ready for presentation, the donor could inscribe the gift with the following verse:

> A little gift by friendship's hand conferred,
> Is often to the costliest gem preferred.

Cassell's Household Guide was an invaluable repository of self-help advice and contained this suggestion for making gifts at home:

ARTICLES FOR GIFTS AND FANCY FAIRS.

Many pretty fancy articles can be made from scraps of ribbon or silk and satin, with the addition of pins, beads, and spangles. Paper spangles are the kind to be used in the articles now described, and can be bought in penny packets at toy shops. Red gold and bright gold spangles are wanted; and a few old playing or writing cards.

The Guitar.—This is a particularly pretty little article. The materials required are a little piece of light, bright-green satin, a very little bit of black gros-grain silk, or ribbon; green, black, and pale yellow, fine sewing-silk; and a little narrow, white, sarcenet ribbon; a few gold and red spangles, some small white pins, and a gold lion of embossed paper, which can be bought where the spangles are sold; also some thin card and a little gum. From the card, cut two pieces like the body of the guitar. Cover these with the green satin, by tacking it one end to the other, across the wrong side. Cut a little piece

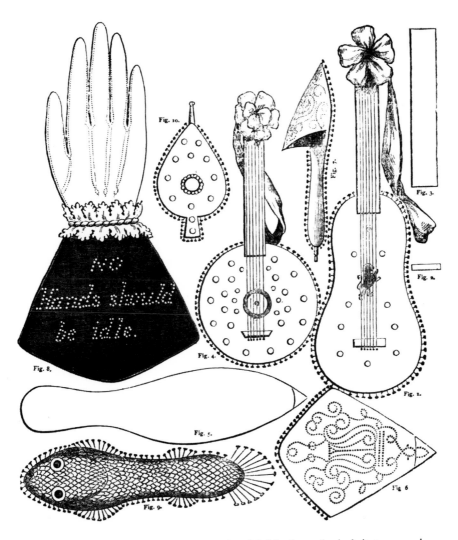

of card, like Fig. 2; cover it very neatly with black, and stitch it to one piece of the body, as the bridge shown in Fig. 1. It must be stitched upright, on end. Cut two pieces of card, like Fig. 3; cover each with black silk, stitch one to the upper piece of the body of the guitar, with invisible stitches. Then with the yellow silk imitate the strings, beginning just beyond the bridge, carrying them over the bridge, up to the top of the back piece. Before putting on the strings, fix the lion in the centre, and the red and gold spangles round it with thick gum, made by melting a little with water, in an egg-cup, by placing it in the oven or on the hob. Neatly stitch the second black piece to the other

21

part of the guitar body. Then sew the two black pieces neatly together with black silk, uniting the tops, and with green silk sew the two pieces of the guitar together. Make a loop of white sarcenet ribbon at the top of the black part, and cover the join with a handsome knot of white bows. To complete it, stick small white pins around the body of the guitar at the edges, between the stitches of the sewing. The colour may be varied, but green is the most effective. The illustrations are of the correct size.

A Mandoline.—Fig. 4 is a mandoline, or banjo. For the latter instrument the round may be smaller. The materials are a little bit of white satin, a little bit of red, some black gros-grain, some narrow, red satin ribbon, a pennyworth of spangles, white and black and yellow sewing silk, and some small white pins; also a little cardboard and gum. Cut two rounds the size of that in Fig. 4, and two straight pieces by the same illustration. Cover both of the latter on one side with black gros-grain. Cover the rounds one with white, the other with cherry-coloured satin, each on one side only. Cut a bridge for the mandoline as for the guitar; cover it with black, and stitch it on. Paint a circle on the white satin to form the hole in the centre, or make it of spangles. Gilt circles can be bought in paper as well as gilt lions. Gum the spangles round the circles. Stitch on one of the black pieces, and then form the strings of the yellow silk. Stitch the other black piece to the red circle. Stitch both black pieces together, and then the circles together with white silk. Stick pins all round the circle only, and make a loop of cherry ribbon, and a handsome knot of bows at the top.

The Turkish Slipper.—Materials: a little cardboard, a couple of old playing or visiting cards, some white silk, coloured satin or velvet, gold and white seed beads, a bodkin, a thimble, and some white pins. Coloured and white sewing silk. Cut in card two pieces of the shape of Fig. 5. Cover each on one side with white silk, and sew them neatly together, leaving a space at the end to insert the bodkin. Cut one piece of very thin card, the shape of Fig. 6. Cover one side with coloured satin or velvet. Work on the pattern in gold and crystal seed beads. Cut white silk the same size, tack it on as a lining, turning a little bit in all round; sew it all round. This finished, make the toe of the slipper. Sew the two long sides of the toe that come to a point to the two sides of the toe part of the sole. Fig. 7 shows the appearance of the complete slipper. Put in the bodkin in the way indicated, and stick small pins, such as the haberdashers use for ribbons, all round the edge of the sole and edge of the front of the toe. Fit the thimble into the toe.

Hand Penwiper.—Materials: a piece of new white card, stout, such as London board, a little piece of black velvet and any fancy material; a little white blond lace, passementerie, chalk seed beads, and black sewing silk. Cut the hand out of the white card. Dot on the glove seams with pen and ink, or omit them. The card is cut a little longer than what is shown in the illustration, Fig. 8, to allow the penwiper to be attached. Cut the shape of the cuff in two pieces, either both of black velvet, or one of velvet and one of fancy material for the wrong side. Work on the motto, "No hands should be idle," to the black velvet with chalk beads. On the wrong side stitch the two cuff pieces together, and turn them. Before attaching them to the hand, cut four pieces out of fancy material a little smaller, and notch the edges. Sew these first to the hand, and the ornamental piece over them. Then run on two pieces of blond lace, one each way at the wrist of the hand, in the way shown in Fig. 8, and between them place a row of passementerie.

Fish Pincushion.—Materials: a small card, a little bit of grey silk, a little bit of Brussels net, a few pins, and a bit of wadding. Cut two cards, the shape of Fig. 9; cover each on one side with grey silk, tacked across the back from edge to edge, every way straining it tight. Colour on one side with Indian ink; draw the eyes, rings round them, the nostrils, and the division of the head. Cover both pieces with white net. Sew the two together; when one side is sewn, put a little wadding between. When nearly sewn all round, stuff in with the scissors more wadding, if wanted. There should be enough to make the fish look as plump as a real one. If a little powder scent is put in with the wadding it is an improvement. Put on the fins and tail with pins in the manner shown in Fig. 9, and between them, all round the fish, place pins close in.

The Bellows.—Materials: card, some silk or satin, some spangles, a bodkin, pins, and sewing silk. Cut two pieces of card, the shape of Fig. 10; cover each on one side with silk or satin—both look best alike; sew them together. Leave open a space for the bodkin, which forms the nose. On the right side fix spangles with gum, a circle in the centre, and the rest dotted about. All round the edge, between the sewing, place pins.

For children, then as now, Christmas was a time for sweets and toys. Although both could be and were bought in vast quantities, the former were often made at home. *Cassell's Household Guide* again gave instructions:

To make Everton Toffee ...

Get one pound of treacle, the same quantity of moist sugar and half a pound of butter. Put them in a saucepan large enough to allow of fast boiling over a clear fire. Put in the butter first and rub it well over the bottom of the saucepan, and add the treacle and the sugar, stirring together gently with a knife. After it has boiled for about ten minutes, ascertain if it is done, in the following way:—Have ready a basin of cold water, and drop a little of the mixture into it from the point of a knife. If it is sufficiently done, when you take it from the water it will be quite crisp. Now prepare a large shallow tin pan, or dish,

Various firms frequently put Christmas advertisements in newspapers and magazines. One of the most popular dolls of 1885 was obviously Miss Dolly Daisy Dimple with a 'travelling trunk full of fine clothes' and costing 'only one shilling' (**10**). Mappin and Webb offered to supply the public direct with the 'largest stock of presents in England' (**11**).

10

THE CRAZE OF THE SEASON.
All Orders are now executed by return of post.
ENGLISH TOYS! FOR CHRISTMAS PRESENTS!
(BY ROYAL LETTERS PATENT.)

Miss Dollie Daisie Dimple

Dressed in her best Walking Costume, with her Travelling Trunk full of fine clothes. Pretty Frocks and Hats in the latest Fashions, to suit all occasions and all seasons. Petticoats, Bodices, Tippets, Skirts, Aprons, Corsets, and a great variety of Underclothing, all to take on and off, and many other pretty things only to be found in a properly appointed Dolly's Outfit.

Together with a little Book all about Miss Dimple's Birthday and early History.

COMPLETE, ONLY ONE SHILLING.

Can be obtained, Retail, from Toy-Dealers, Fancy Bazaars, Stationers, and others, everywhere. Sole Wholesale Agents for the World,

Messrs. HINDE,
LONDON, BIRMINGHAM,
and PARIS.

The Trunk and Contents will be sent, carriage paid, for 15 stamps, from HINDE'S London Sample-Room, 1a, CITY-ROAD, E.C. Applicants' Addresses should be distinctly written.
The money will be returned willingly, if any dissatisfaction; and as an additional guarantee of the bonâ fide nature of this wonderful shilling's-worth, samples will be submitted to the Editors of the various Publications in which the announcements appear.
N.B.—It is specially important that the Name and Add-ess be written clearly, as Messrs. Hinde have in their possession several hundreds of letters in which not only the name, but address, has been omitted. Should this come under the notice of any of the readers of these incomplete orders, they are requested to communicate, with the view of identifying the same.

11

MAPPIN & WEBB, WHOLESALE MANUFACTURERS, Supply the Public Direct.

PRESENTS FOR THE SEASON

THE LARGEST STOCK OF PRESENTS IN ENGLAND.

AT MANUFACTURERS' WHOLESALE PRICES.

PRESENTS FOR THE SEASON

ILLUSTRATED CATALOGUES FREE.

rubbed all over with butter, to prevent its adhering, and into this pour the toffee from the saucepan to get cold, when it can be easily removed. To keep it good, it should be excluded from the air.

To make peppermint drops ...

Mix half a pound of sifted sugar into sufficient lemon juice to make it a proper thickness. Dry it over a fire, gently stirring in, at the same time, one hundred and twenty drops of the oil of peppermint; after which, drop the mixture upon white paper well greased.

And although some simple toys were home-made, the vast majority were bought. Victorian London abounded with toy shops and bazaars, and the inventiveness of the toymaker grew with the years of the century.

Until the third decade of the twentieth century, the centre of toy making had always been in Germany. With the growth of emigration to America, however, German manufacturers spread their skills into the New World, while Englishmen like Frank Hornby and William Britain began to establish a reputation for English toys. But for the Victorian child toys very often came from German workshops and the variety they offered was quite remarkable.

For girls there were dolls—dolls to dress and dolls to play with, Dutch dolls and golliwogs, dolls with porcelain heads and fabric or leather-covered bodies. Many came with whole wardrobes and outfits for every activity. And, of course, there were dolls' houses. Some were simple playthings, but many were perfect architectural miniatures of actual houses complete from footscraper to chimney. No doubt Victorian parents derived almost as much pleasure from some toys as their children did.

Overleaf: Further evidence of the variety of Victorian Christmas presents can be seen in the following advertisements by major stores and manufacturers in the 1890s. Alexander Clark offered silver presents ranging from a boot match stand to a blotting book (not forgetting the new aromatic scent ball charm) (**12**). Peter Robinson had some 'delightful toys' for sale (**13**). D. H. Evans's 'Christmas Bazaar' included cases, calendars and candlestick-holders (**14**) and all kinds of toys and trinklets, both moveable and static, were on view at Shoolbred's (**15**). Department stores still announce their wares in the same way in modern newspapers and magazines.

NEW STYLE SOLID SILVER WAIST CLASP.

SOLID SILVER HAIR BRUSH.

NEW ARO-MATIC SCENT BALL CHARM.

SILVER BLOTTING BOOK.

SOLID SILVER SAFETY TRAVELLING INKSTAND.

SOLID SILVER MIRROR.

ROMAN LAMP CIGAR LIGHTER.

COMBINATION PURSE AND CARD CASE.

SOLID SILVER HAT BRUSH.

SILVER SHOE PINCUSHION.

SOLID SILVER BOOT MATCH STAND.

THE NEW WATCH PHOTOGRAPH.

SILVER PURSE.

LIQUEUR FRAME: SILVER-MOUNTED JUGS AND GLASSES.

MANICURE SET IN SOLID SILVER.

LAMP AND POWDER-BOX COMBINED.

CHRISTMAS NOVELTIES AT THE ALEXANDER CLARK MANUFACTURING COMPANY'S.

12

CHRISMAS BAZAAR AT D. H. EVANS'S.

CHRISTMAS PRESENTS
AT SHOOLBRED'S.

15

For boys the choice was wider still. Victorian mechanical ingenuity had produced working models in miniature of almost everything a child might experience in the real world outside the nursery. There were trains and boats, carriages and coaches. There were toy soldiers and forts to put them in, toy firemen and fire engines for them to drive. And, of course, there were games, games of chance and skill, from Snakes and Ladders to Happy Families. The market was enormous, and the huge number of toy museums all over the world bear witness to the vast and varied number of playthings with which our ancestors regaled their offspring on Christmas Day.

In many continental countries and indeed in most countries in the Christian World, it was customary to give and receive presents on New Year's Day or on St Nicholas' Day (6 December). But in England in the nineteenth century it became the custom to exchange presents on Christ-

No child can resist a toy for Christmas, and it was as true for the Victorians as it is today. The inventiveness and ingenuity of Victorian toymakers was remarkable. Assembled here are photographs of some of the highly intricate models and 'mechanical marvels' which no doubt gave as much pleasure to the Victorian giver of presents as to the recipient. The musical pig is very nattily dressed (**16**). A particularly attractive gift must have been this painting clown (**17**) who drew a picture on the easel when one of the templates was inserted at the side. Among these templates were a portrait of Gladstone and one of Harlequin. The painted cast-iron model of a hansom cab (**18**) was designed to be pulled along the floor by a child (c. 1875). The toy theatre (**19**) was similar to the kind made, and still being made by Pollocks of London. The printed figures and scenery were cut out and applied to wooden backings. The brass and copper steam-powered train (**20**) was made about 1880. A Christmas present of 1891 was the nickel-plated model (**21**) of a Merryweather fire engine made to hold cigarettes and matches. And last, but not least, every boy's dream was to have some model soldiers (**22**) or a replica of a sailing ship (**23**).

16

17

18

19

20

21

22

23

mas Day itself: in some circles, apparently, even on Christmas Eve. As Albert, Prince Consort, wrote to his father in 1841,

> This is the dear Christmas Eve, on which I have so often listened with impatience for your step, which was to usher us into the present room. Today I have two children of my own to give presents to ...

But no matter when the presents were given, and no matter what they cost, the Victorians were adamant on one point. It was the thought that counted. As the poetess Ella Wheeler Wilcox put it: '...it is not Art, but Heart, which wins the wide world over.' The humblest home-made gift was more precious than a casquet of jewels; the child's sampler worked with love more treasured than silver or gold. The Victorians had only to open any collection of popular verse to see their convictions on this point firmly corroborated by George R. Sims. His famous poem, 'Billy's Rose', tells of one seasonal gift that was beyond the price of rubies in terms of the cost to the giver. One contemporary critic found the sentiments

33

expressed wholly admirable: 'To our mind, at least, a poem such as "Billy's Rose" is worth a whole hecatomb of more pretentious verse.' And it would undoubtedly have brought a blush to Jo March's face:

BILLY'S ROSE.

Billy's dead, and gone to glory—so is Billy's sister Nell:
There's a tale I know about them were I poet I would tell;
Soft it comes, with perfume laden, like a breath of country air
Wafted down the filthy alley, bringing fragrant odours there.

In that vile and filthy alley, long ago one winter's day,
Dying quick of want and fever, hapless, patient Billy lay,
While beside him sat his sister, in the garret's dismal gloom,
Cheering with her gentle presence Billy's pathway to the tomb.

Many a tale of elf and fairy did she tell the dying child,
Till his eyes lost half their anguish, and his worn, wan features smiled:
Tales herself had heard hap-hazard, caught amid the Babel roar,
Lisped about by tiny gossips playing round their mothers' door.

Then she felt his wasted fingers tighten feebly as she told
How beyond this dismal alley lay a land of shining gold,
Where, when all the pain was over—where, when all the tears were shed—
He would be a white-frocked angel, with a gold thing on his head.

Then she told some garbled story of a kind-eyed Saviour's love,
How He'd built for little children great big playgrounds up above,
Where they sang and played at hop-scotch and at horses all the day,
And where beadles and policemen never frightened them away.

This was Nell's idea of Heaven—just a bit of what she'd heard,
With a little bit invented, and a little bit inferred.
But her brother lay and listened, and he seemed to understand,
For he closed his eyes and murmured he could see the Promised Land.

'Yes,' he whispered, 'I can see it—I can see it, sister Nell;
Oh, the children look so happy, and they're all so strong and well;
I can see them there with Jesus—He is playing with them, too!
Let us run away and join them if there's room for me and you.'

She was eight, this little maiden, and her life had all been spent
In the garret and the alley, where they starved to pay the rent;
Where a drunken father's curses and a drunken mother's blows
Drove her forth into the gutter from the day's dawn to its close.

But she knew enough, this outcast, just to tell the sinking boy,
'You must die before you're able all these blessings to enjoy.
You must die,' she whispered, 'Billy, and I am not even ill;
But I'll come to you, dear brother,—yes, I promise that I will.'

'You are dying, little brother,—you are dying, oh, so fast;
I heard father say to mother that he knew you couldn't last.
They will put you in a coffin, then you'll wake and be up there,
While I'm left alone to suffer in this garret bleak and bare.'

'Yes, I know it,' answered Billy. 'Ah, but, sister, I don't mind,
Gentle Jesus will not beat me; He's not cruel or unkind.
But I can't help thinking, Nelly, I should like to take away
Something, sister, that you gave me, I might look at every day.

'In the summer you remember how the mission took us out
To a great green lovely meadow, where we played and ran about,
And the van that took us halted by a sweet bright patch of land,
Where the fine red blossoms grew, dear, half as big as mother's hand.

'Nell, I asked the good kind teacher what they called such flowers as those,
And he told me, I remember, that the pretty name was rose.
I had never seen them since, dear—how I wish that I had one!
Just to keep and think of you, Nell, when I'm up beyond the sun.'

Not a word said little Nelly; but at night, when Billy slept,
On she flung her scanty garments and then down the stairs she crept.
Through the silent streets of London she ran nimbly as a fawn,
Running on and running ever till the night had changed to dawn.

When the foggy sun had risen, and the mist had cleared away,
All around her, wrapped in snowdrift, there the open country lay.
She was tired, her limbs were frozen, and the roads had cut her feet,
But there came no flowery gardens her poor tearful eyes to greet.

She had traced the road by asking—she had learnt the way to go;
She had found the famous meadow—it was wrapped in cruel snow;

Not a buttercup or daisy, not a single verdant blade
Showed its head above its prison. Then she knelt her down and prayed.

With her eyes upcast to heaven, down she sank upon the ground,
And she prayed to God to tell her where the roses might be found.
Then the cold blast numbered her senses, and her sight grew strangely dim;
And a sudden, awful tremor seemed to seize her every limb.

'Oh, a rose!' she moaned, 'good Jesus—just a rose to take to Bill!'
And as she prayed a chariot came thundering down the hill;
And a lady sat there, toying with a red rose, rare and sweet;
As she passed she flung it from her, and it fell at Nelly's feet.

Just a word her lord had spoken caused her ladyship to fret,
And the rose had been his present, so she flung it in a pet;
But the poor, half-blinded Nelly thought it fallen from the skies,
And she murmured, 'Thank you, Jesus!' as she clasped the dainty prize.

Lo that night from out the alley did a child's soul pass away,
From dirt and sin and misery to where God's children play.
Lo that night a wild, fierce snowstorm burst in fury o'er the land,
And at morn they found Nell frozen, with the red rose in her hand.

Billy's dead, and gone to glory—so is Billy's sister Nell;
Am I bold to say this happened in the land where angels dwell:—
That the children met in heaven, after all their earthly woes,
And that Nelly kissed her brother, and said, 'Billy, here's your rose'?

Christmas Cards.

Very happy may it be
Christmas time to thine and thee.

CHRISTMAS CARD GREETING,
c. 1884

AT THE end of the winter term eighteenth-century schoolmasters would set their pupils to work on their 'Christmas Pieces'. These were samplers of writing and writing exercises on superior paper with engraved borders designed to show parents how their little ones had progressed during the year. Children continued to work their 'Christmas Pieces' well into the nineteenth century, but by about 1820 the engraved borders were enhanced by colour and the children's productions were much more decorative. These offerings were the forerunners of the great Victorian Christmas Card which made its first appearance in 1843.

In that year Sir Henry Cole commissioned John Calcott Horsley, a member of the Royal Academy, to design for him a Christmas card which would obviate the necessity of writing letters to each and every one of his large circle of friends and family. This card was issued from the office of a contemporary periodical—*Felix Summerley's Home Treasury*—and sold for a shilling a copy. Lithographed and hand-coloured, it portrayed a family party of three generations quaffing wine—which caused a mild furore among the temperate classes!—flanked on either side by allegorical vignettes depicting the feeding of the hungry and the clothing of the naked. The whole was enclosed in a rustic frame of gnarled wood and ivy and the greeting ran, 'A merry Christmas and a Happy New Year to You'.

In 1844 Mr W. C. T. Dobson produced a sketch symbolizing the 'Spirit of Christmas', which sold many more than the one thousand that Horsley's had. The novelty was beginning to catch on. In 1848 Mr W. M. Edgley's card repeated much the same scene as Horsley's in much the same rustic frame. His card, however, depicted holly for the first time, although he balanced this modern touch with a suitably archaic spelling in the greeting: 'A merry Christmass and a Happy New Year to You'.

From these somewhat slow beginnings the vast business of Victorian Christmas cards grew. Sales proliferated as did designs and sizes. Cards were bell-shaped, circular, fan-shaped, oval, crescent-shaped and diamond. There were folding cards, jewelled cards, irridescent cards, embossed cards, cards with verses, cards with carols and cards with simple greetings:

> Love and Peace with thee abide
> Through the holy Christmastide!

The popular, late Victorian lyric writer, Frederic E. Weatherley, was not above contributing a greeting for a commercial card: 'But not mottoes for crackers, I drew the line there!' Certainly cracker mottoes cramped the

24 The first Christmas card, designed in 1843 for Sir Henry Cole by John Calcott Horsley, a member of the Royal Academy.

25 Four Christmas cards from the 1860s.

26 A collage of humorous Christmas cards (1877).

27 A Christmas card, illustrating a curious facet of the Victorian sense of humour (*c.* 1870).

28 Two late Victorian cards reflecting the aesthetic movement of the late nineteenth century.

Victorian poet's style, but verses on Christmas cards could be quite expansive and, above all, moral, as can be seen from the following:

Oh, Life is but a river;
And in our childhood, we
But a fair running streamlet
Adorn'd with flowers see.

But as we grow more earnest,
The river grows more deep;
And where we laugh'd in childhood,
We, older, pause to weep.

Each Christmas as it passes,
Some change to us doth bring;
Yet to our friends the closer,
As Time creeps on, we cling.

29 Two designs for Christmas cards by Kate Greenaway.

30 The influence of the Arts and Crafts movement and the private presses of the late Victorian period is clearly shown in this card.

The materials that cards were made of became as varied as their shapes as the century progressed. Satin, silk, plush and brocade were used just as much as lace and embroidery. Designs, too, were at least as varied as they are today. Landscapes in either winter or summer, seascapes and floral decorations were just as acceptable as religious subjects or portrayals of Father Christmas.

From Horsley's simple first card to the lavish productions of the 1880s was a mere forty years, but sales figures were, by then, well into the millions as can be seen from the huge number of Victorian Christmas cards which have survived into our modern throwaway age.

By the end of the nineteenth century, therefore, Christmas cards were

31 A private Christmas card commissioned from H. F. New in 1889.

32 An 1896 Christmas card.

such an established fact of life that George and Weedon Grossmith felt obliged to make reference to one in their celebrated *Diary of a Nobody*. Mr Pooter opens his mail on 24 December:

> I am a poor man, but I would gladly give ten shillings to find out who sent me the insulting Christmas card I received this morning. I never insult people; why should they insult me? The worst part of the transaction is, that I find myself suspecting all my friends. The handwriting on the envelope is evidently disguised, being written sloping the wrong way. I cannot think either Gowing or Cummings would do such a mean thing. Lupin denied all knowledge of it, and I believe him; although I disapprove of him laughing and sympathising with the offender. Mr Franching would be above such an act; and I don't think any of the Mutlars would descend to such a course. I wonder if Pitt, that impudent clerk at the office, did it? Or Mrs Birrell, the charwoman, or Burwin-Fosselton? The writing is too good for the former.

Mr Pooter tantalizingly omits to describe his 'insulting' card, but the designs of many Victorian Christmas cards were bizarre in the extreme. Cards imported from Germany were complete with moving sections and depicted such inappropriate scenes as a schoolmaster chastising a pupil, and in one extreme example a husband murdering his wife. The only seasonal thing about such cards is a jaunty 'Merry Christmas' pasted on to the foot almost as an afterthought. Such cards would certainly have found favour in certain quarters of Victorian society where the border between a sense of humour and a sense of the macabre was a thin one. For the most part, however, the designs for Christmas cards were drawn from more seasonal topics although religious cards were never so numerous as one might have expected. There were always more robins than angels.

Sending Christmas cards was certainly not cheap for the Victorian family. Mr Horsley's card had cost a shilling, and while thinking longingly of the penny black stamp, one must remember how much one penny could buy at the time. However, if the sender answered the Postmaster-General's call to 'post early' he could be sure that his card would arrive in time for the day, for the postman delivered mail every morning—even on Christmas Day itself.

Christmas Decorations.

◆

The damsel donn'd her kirtle sheen;
The hall was dress'd with holly green;
Forth to the wood did merry-men go,
To gather in the mistletoe.

Christmas Eve in the Olden Time
SIR WALTER SCOTT

◆

THE origin of the custom of decorating houses with greenery at festivals is hidden in the mists of time. Pope Gregory I in a famous letter to Augustine at Canterbury advised him to encourage such of the local customs as were capable of a Christian interpretation. And so it was that even mistletoe, most sacred to our pagan ancestors, was allowed to remain in our homes and even on occasions in our churches with the full blessing of the Pope and doubtless the silent approval of hovering druid spirits!

Christmas decoration was not invented by the Victorians, but it was a custom which they enriched with their own inventiveness and enthusiasm. *Cassell's Household Guide* provided detailed instructions for 'Christmas Decorations of the Home' which are just as applicable today.

> The materials to be used include all kinds of evergreens, everlasting flowers, and coloured and gilt papers ... No Christmas would be thought complete if there did not hang in hall or dining-room a bunch of mistletoe with its curiously forked branches, with their terminal pairs of nerveless pale-green leaves and white crystalline berries.
>
> Holly is of course the special tree of the season. Its leaves bent into various curves, its thorny points, and its bunches of coral-red berries, make it the prince of evergreens. Let it be conspicuous throughout the decorations. It is a good plan to strip off the berries, and use them strung in bunches, as the berries get hidden when the sprigs are worked into wreaths and devices, and the berries, bent into little bunches, dotted about the festoons here and there, look very effective.

46

33 Decorating the family portrait (1871).

34 A Victorian drawing room decorated for Christmas (*c.* 1890).

35 A countryman and his family gathering evergreens for Christmas decorations (1871).

Ivy must be introduced with care. Small single leaves come in with good effect in small devices, or to relieve a background of sombre yew or arbor vitae. The young shoots of the common ivy are best, or of the kind which grows up trees and old walls, which are very dark and glossy, with a network of light-coloured veins. Laurel is a very useful green in sprays, and the single leaves may be applied with excellent effect in wreaths or overlapping one another in borders. The variegated ancuba makes a pleasing variety in the colour.

Yews and arbor vitae are useful, especially the small sprays of them, for covering the framework of devices.

Myrtle and box also are pretty in narrow borderings, into which coloured everlasting flowers may be introduced. The black bunches of ivy berries may sometimes be used with advantage, to give points of contrast in the decorations. Of course if chrysanthemums, Christmas roses, primulas, and camellias can be obtained, the general effect is heightened and the decoration becomes more elaborate and more elegant.

The best wreaths for decorating the banisters of a house, or any pedestals, pillars, or columns, are those made in a rope of evergreen sprigs.

There are several ways in which such wreaths are made. One way is as follows:

Get a rope or stout cord of proper length, and a quantity of twine and a handful of evergreen twigs. Begin at one end of the rope, which should be attached firmly to something. Dispose a bunch of the twigs round the rope, and tie them on with the twine; then dispose another bunch so that the leaves may conceal the stalks of those already on, and give the twine a turn round them, fastening it with a running knot, and so on until the rope is finished. This must be done at the fastening of each bunch of twigs. Another way very frequently adopted is, in place of a rope, to use only a piece of stout twine to run through the wreath, so as to prevent its falling to pieces, and, instead of twine to tie the twigs on, to use fine wire, which must be firmly twisted around the twigs.

In fastening the wreath to the pillars, take care not to put it on upside down, as foliage must never be placed in a direction contrary to that of its growth. When small chaplets or wreaths are constructed, each should be made by one person, as the effect is frequently spoilt by the two ends not matching, or it is otherwise wanting in uniformity. When the wreaths are finished, and before they are hung up, they should be kept in some cool place, or else they shrivel up; if necessary, a *little* water may be sprinkled over them.

If there is a lamp in the dining-room, supported by chains, holly wreaths twisted round the chains look well; while a chaplet round the base, and a small basket filled with mistletoe, suspended from the centre of the base, look very effective. Borders of evergreens may be placed along the back of the sideboard, and if there be a mirror in it a small chaplet in the centre, and seeming to join the borders, looks very pretty. Pictures and mirrors can be framed with made-up borders of evergreens. Where these are square, borders arranged in the shape of Oxford frames look very pretty. If the entrance-hall be in panels, narrow borderings of box and ivy look well, laid on all round, and in the centre half hoops or chaplets, or a monogram. Scrolls, with mottoes, bidding people to be welcome and happy, either laid on bright-coloured calicoes, with holly borderings, or else merely the word "Christmas," done in laurel leaves, and variegated with immortelle flowers. Even in the bedrooms the frames of pictures and mirrors can be edged with wreaths.

Fig. 1.

Fig. 2.

Fig. 3.

Fig. 4.

In Fig. 4 will be found a bold and effective device for a large space, as, for example, the end wall of an entrance-hall or landing. The cross pieces are stout sticks, the size of which must be regulated by the space intended to be filled; and it will be found advisable to join them in the centre by a cross joint, otherwise they will be very awkward to manage. They can then be wreathed with holly and mistletoe, as shown in the figure. The legend surrounding them is made of letters in gilt paper, pasted on to coloured cardboard, and the figure of the robin is cut out in cardboard and painted.

The monogram in Fig. 2, signifies Christmas, and is very pretty made either of leaves and berries, or moss, glued on cardboard, and edged with three different shades of immortelles. The border is made of bosses of different coloured immortelles, and the outside row of star points with fern fronds. Fig. 1 is a bordering for the cornice of a hall, or large room, and is made of laurel leaves and rosettes of coloured paper or immortelles. In Fig. 3 the trefoil is made of holly leaves, and the border of laurel.

In our decorations we must not forget the dining-room table when our guests gather round it. A very pretty centre-piece is made by covering an inverted basin with moss, into which insert sprigs of holly quite thick until it forms a pyramid of holly. On the top place a figure of Old Father Christmas (which may be bought at any bazaar or sugar-plum shop), and instead of the holly sprig he generally holds in his hand, place a spray of mistletoe.

A great many lights are required, where fir and holly are much used, in table decoration, otherwise the effect is heavy and gloomy.

These hints will make it an easy task to adorn the house for Christmas; but half the pleasure consists in inventing new devices, and giving scope to one's taste and ingenuity, new ideas springing up and developing themselves as the occasion arises, till the worker finds delight in the work, and is thus best rewarded for the toil.

Before the advent of the Christmas tree, mistletoe, in some arrangement like the kissing bunch—two hoops set to make a sphere, decorated with greenery, oranges, and apples—was the centrepiece of Christmas decorations in the Victorian home. And even after its establishment, the Christmas tree did not oust the witness of so many shy maidens' first kisses. In *Pickwick Papers*, Charles Dickens describes the scene under the mistletoe on Christmas Eve in Mr Wardle's kitchen:

From the centre of the ceiling of this kitchen, old Wardle had just suspended with his own hands a huge branch of mistletoe, and this same branch of mistletoe instantaneously gave rise to a scene of general and most delightful strug-

36 For those who could not get their own holly from the countryside, a holly cart
came round the streets just before Christmas (1848).

37 Children gathering mistletoe (1851).

38 A mistletoe seller calls at the gate of Myrtle Lodge (1853).

gling and confusion; in the midst of which Mr. Pickwick with a gallantry which would have done honour to a descendant of Lady Trollimglower herself, took the old lady by the hand, led her beneath the mystic branch, and saluted her in all courtesy and decorum. The old lady submitted to this piece of practical politeness with all the dignity which befitted so important and serious a solemnity, but the younger ladies not being so thoroughly imbued with a superstitious veneration of the custom, or imagining that the value of a salute is very much enhanced if it cost a little trouble to obtain it, screamed and struggled, and ran into corners, and threatened and remonstrated, and did everything but leave the room, until some of the less adventurous gentlemen were on the point of desisting, when they all at once found it useless to resist any longer, and submitted to be kissed with a good grace. Mr. Winkle kissed the young lady with the black eyes, and Mr. Snodgrass kissed Emily; and Mr. Weller, not being particular about the form of being under the mistletoe, kissed Emma and the other female servants, just as he caught them. As to the poor relations, they kissed everybody, not even excepting the plainer portion of the young-lady visitors, who, in their excessive confusion, ran right under the mistletoe, directly it was hung up, without knowing it! Wardle stood with his back to the fire, surveying the whole scene, with the utmost satisfaction; and the fat boy took the opportunity of appropriating to his own use, and summarily devouring, a particularly fine mince-pie, that had been carefully put by for somebody else.

Now the screaming had subsided, and faces were in a glow and curls in a tangle, and Mr. Pickwick, after kissing the old lady as before mentioned, was standing under the mistletoe, looking with a very pleased countenance on all that was passing around him, when the young lady with the black eyes, after a little whispering with the other young ladies, made a sudden dart forward, and, putting her arm around Mr. Pickwick's neck, saluted him affectionately on the left cheek; and before Mr. Pickwick distinctly knew what was the matter, he was surrounded by the whole body, and kissed by every one of them.

And Cuthbert Bede, in winsome mood, dedicated a poem in 1855 to 'Mistletoe Morning':

> 'Twas mistletoe morning,
> And Chanticleer's warning
> Had summoned fine folks from their beds and their blankets:
> When I saw in a vision
> Of Dreamland elysian,
> A bevy of Cupids swarm forth for their prankets.
> There was fun in their faces,
> As all took their places,
> And link'd themselves laughingly—mad little frolickers;
> And never such laughter
> Shook roof, beam, and rafter,
> As shook the fat sides of these roystering rolickers.
>
> With unfettered actions
> They formed in two factions,

39 Putting up the holly and mistletoe (1855).

And, nude as old statues, selected their places;
    Little rosy carousers,
    Without any trousers,
And quite independent of straps and of braces.
    Such tints were their limbs on,
    Such hues of rich crimson,
Such roses, and lilies, wax apples, and cherries,
    That they gleamed hot and sunny,
    As, with frolickings funny,
They snowballed each other with mistletoe berries!

Prince Albert is credited with the establishing of the Christmas tree in England. In fact Queen Charlotte, the wife of George III, had set up a tree at Windsor in the eighteenth century, but it was after 1841 when Prince

Albert imported trees from Coburg that the fashion really caught on. The *Illustrated London News* of 1845 described the erection of a Christmas tree in Cripplegate, London:

> A very pleasing celebration of the season was given by the London Mission Society, at the Temperance Hall in Milton Street, City... As many as 400 children assembled in the Hall, with their teachers and friends; and, whoever saw their happy little faces, and heard their shouts, needs no further proof of their enjoyment, which was crowned especially by the exhibition of a German Christmas Tree or Tree of Love, which was erected upon the stage of the Hall. This is the usual mode of celebrating the Eve of the birth of Christ in Germany and on the continent. In almost every family, is set up this pleasing figure, having the resemblance of a growing tree, loaded with a profusion of fruits and flowers; and, upon its branches, the different members of the family suspend the little presents which they intend for those they love the best; and on the exhibition of the tree, the presents are claimed by the donors, and handed, with compliments, to their friends.
>
> On Wednesday evening, the children of the Mission hung a load of oranges and other fruit on their Christmas tree, besides hundreds of other presents; the whole being illuminated with a myriad of candles.

And *The Dictionary of Daily Wants* of 1858 explained the German custom in detail:

> The custom of having illuminated trees at Christmas, laden with pretty little trifles, as momentoes to be presented to the guests of the Christmas party, is derived from Germany. A young fir is generally selected for the Christmas Tree, and little presents of various kinds are bound on the branches, as, crochet-purses, bonbons, preserved fruits, alum-baskets, charms, dolls, toys in endless variety etc., distributed over the tree according to fancy. The whole is illuminated by numerous little wax tapers, which are lighted just before the guests are admitted to inspect the tree. Before the tapers are quite burnt out the guests all assemble around the tree, and the souvenirs are taken off and presented to the guests whose names have either been previously appended to them, or at the discretion of the distributor.

Prince Albert's innovation had certainly caught the public imagination and the 'German' Christmas tree quickly became established as the centrepiece of all seasonal decoration. The brightness of the little candles and

40 Taking advantage of the mistletoe (1846).

41 *Top right:* A Christmas kiss for Papa (1865) ...

42 ... and one for Grandfather (1863).

the excitement of the children who waited around it to claim their presents were described by many Victorian writers including Charles Dickens:

A CHRISTMAS TREE.

I have been looking on, this evening, at a merry company of children assembled round that pretty German toy, a Christmas Tree. The tree was planted in the middle of a great round table, and towered high above their heads. It was brilliantly lighted by a multitude of little tapers; and everywhere sparkled and glittered with bright objects. There were rosy-cheeked dolls, hiding behind the green leaves; and there were real watches (with movable hands, at least, and an endless capacity of being wound up) dangling from innumerable twigs; there were French-polished tables, chairs, bedsteads, wardrobes, eight-day clocks, and various other articles of domestic furniture (wonderfully made, in tin, at Wolverhampton), perched among the boughs, as if in preparation for some fairy housekeeping; there were jolly, broad-faced little men, much more agreeable in appearance than many real men—and no wonder, for their heads took off, and showed them to be full of sugar-plums; there were fiddles and drums; there were tambourines, books, work-boxes, paint-boxes, sweetmeat-boxes, peep-show boxes, and all kinds of boxes; there were trinkets for the elder girls, far brighter than any grown-up gold and jewels; there were baskets and pincushions in all devices; there were guns, swords, and banners; there were witches standing in enchanted rings of pasteboard, to tell fortunes; there were teetotums, humming-tops, needle-cases, pen-wipers, smelling-bottles, conversation-cards, bouquet-holders; real fruit, made artificially dazzling with goldleaf; imitation apples, pears, and walnuts, crammed with surprises; in short, as a pretty child, before me, delightedly whispered to another pretty child, her bosom friend, 'There was everything, and more.' This motley collection of odd objects, clustering on the tree like magic fruit, and flashing back the bright looks directed towards it from every side—some of the diamond-eyes admiring it were hardly on a level with the table, and a few were languishing in timid wonder on the bosoms of pretty mothers, aunts, and nurses—made a lively realisation of the fancies of childhood; and set me thinking how all the trees that grow and all the things that come into existence on the earth, have their wild adornments at that well-remembered time.

43 The chosen tree (1851).

44 One of the first English Christmas trees (*c.* 1845).

45 The Royal Family stands around the Christmas tree at Windsor Castle (1848).

ARTICLES FOR CHRISTMAS-TREES.

A CHRISTMAS-TREE may be made at home for a very trifling cost. Long as they have been in fashion in England for juvenile parties, or for Christmas-eve, these trees seem to be still in favour almost as much as ever. Christmas-trees may be covered with paltry trifles, or made the medium of dispensing suitable gifts amongst the members of a household. When the latter plan is to be adopted, each article is to be marked with the name of the intended recipient. It is also very well to add a few boxes of sugar-plums and valueless trifles, which can afterwards be raffled for. The ordinary Christmas-tree is covered with miscellaneous articles, some of more value than others, which are either distributed at hazard by the coloured paper. Fold the square in half, like Fig. 2, and cut off the piece at the top, making the two sides equal. When opened it will resemble Fig. 3. Gum it as far as the dotted line, and join it. Be sure to join it so that there is not a hole at the point. If it is made of white paper, cut some strips of red, of green, and of gold paper. Edge it with gold, and paste strips of red, green, and gold round it spirally at intervals. If the cone is made of coloured paper, use gold, white, and some favourably contrasting hue. Fig. 4 illustrates it. Another pretty way to make a rather superior ornament is, to cut a cone of bright green satin-paper, and join it. Cut a scarlet tassel, and fasten it at the point. To the top gum a piece of scarlet sarcenet, with a mouth like a bag, and over the join run some blond lace ; turn a row each way,

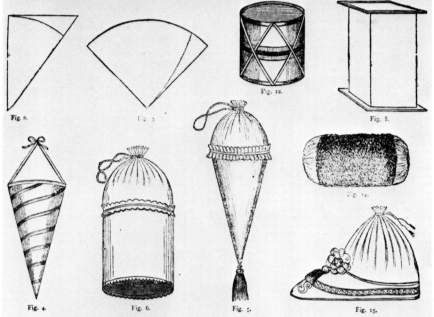

Fig. 2. Fig. 3. Fig. 12. Fig. 8. Fig. 4. Fig. 6. Fig. 5. Fig. 14. Fig. 15.

lady deputed to cut them down, or lots are drawn out of a bag of numbers corresponding to those fixed on the little presents themselves. A good-sized fir-tree, of regular shape, and with nice wide-spreading arms, is wanted. Cover this at regular intervals with gelatine lights, which are better and safer than wax tapers. These lights are like ordinary night-lights, each one contained in a little cup of gay-coloured gelatine, resembling the glass lamps used at illuminations when gas is not employed. Take care to place these lights so that not one of them is put under a bough, which it may set alight. Suspend them by fine wire, not cotton or string, which will take fire. A little behind every light arrange a bright tin reflector, star, or silvered glass ball. A number of flags are requisite to add to the gaiety of the tree, which a few bows of coloured ribbon will also enhance.

A good many small ornamental paper boxes and cases holding sugar-plums will add well to the decorations of the tree. To make paper cones, cut squares in white or and gum a strip of gold paper between (see Fig. 5). Fig. 6 is another kind of sugar-plum case. Cut a straight piece of card, and sew it together to make a round like a drum. Cut a circular piece to fit one end. Cover the sides round with paper, notch the edges, and turn them down at one end over the piece fitted in, and, if well gummed, they will keep it in place. The other end may be first sewed in. Cut a round piece of coloured paper, and gum on lastly at the end. Have a bag-top of some different shade of silk or satin, and gum it on with some pretty piece of passementerie or gilt paper over the join. If the box is covered with straw-colour, and the bag is of blue satin, it will look pretty. Odds and ends of ribbon may be used in making up these little boxes. A more valuable case may be made by first constructing a box of a strip of card, goring it with a strip of paper each side instead of by sewing. Cover this with white paper. When quite dry, bind both edges with blue satin ribbon. Then draw, in water-colours, a garland of flowers round

47 Continuing its series of instructive articles, *Cassell's Household Guide* tells its readers how to make decorations for the Christmas tree.

the barrel. Very neatly sew a blue satin bag at each end. Put a little powdered scent in, enough wadding to fill the bags, and place it on the tree. .It may be suspended by its own strings of blue ribbon. A pedestal is a good design for a fancy case. A design for one is given in Fig. 8. To construct it, take a piece of card large enough to allow for its four sides. Cut this like Fig. 1, allowing four equal sides and a bit over; half-cut through the dotted lines on the right side. Join it round with the small piece inside, and fix it with strong gum. Cut a square larger than the pedestal, for the base. Turn under the little pieces that may be noticed at the base in Fig. 10, below the dotted line, gum them, and fix on the base. For the lid, cut a piece like the base, and a second piece like Fig. 10. Half-cut through the dotted lines. Join the

and fit them into the drum. For the other end cut a similar piece, put a loop of thread or ribbon in the centre, and put it in without gumming it. Made in card, ornamented, filled with sweetmeats, and a piece of net gummed at the top, with a band of gold paper over the join, it is very pretty.

Fig. 14 is a *Muff.*—Make this of a bit of plush that looks like fur. Put a shallow, red silk bag-mouth at each end, to look like the lining. Draw up one and sew it. Cut a piece of paper the size of the muff, roll it round, and slip it inside to keep the muff out stiff. Cardboard can be used instead of paper. Put in the sugar-plums, and draw up the mouth.

The Lucky Shoe (Fig. 15).—Cut a shoe by Fig. 16, of any pretty material; join it and bind it neatly. Cut a sole by

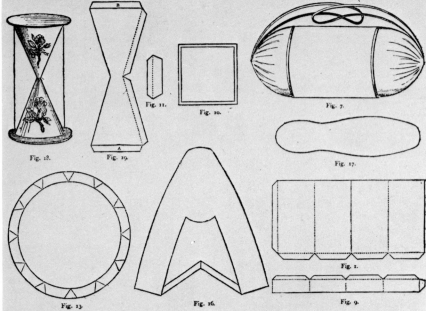

Fig. 11.

Fig. 10.

Fig. 7.

Fig. 18.

Fig. 19.

Fig. 17.

Fig. 13.

Fig. 16.

Fig. 1.

Fig. 9.

piece as the pedestal was joined, and fix the top to this piece in a similar way to that used in joining the base. But Fig. 9 must be a little narrower each side than Fig. 1, so that the smaller piece, Fig. 9, may neatly fit just inside the larger, Fig. 1. Another way to make this is to cut two pieces like Fig. 1, one just small enough to fit inside the other, and fix square ends of equal size to each. To close the box, put one inside another. Ornament the outer one with coloured paper, and bind the edges with gold, or merely bind the edges and draw a group of flowers on each side in water-colours, and also on the lid.

Fig. 12, a *Drum*, can be made of paper, and ornamented with strips of red and of gold paper, and have a few sugar-plums inside. To make it, join a piece of paper as for Fig. 6. Draw, with a bow-pencil, a round as large as the top, and a second round a little larger. Cut out the larger round, and notch the edges up (Fig. 13). When you have done this, turn down the edges, gum them,

Fig. 17. Before joining the upper part, see that it fits the sole well. Cut the sole of card, and tack the material over it. Sew the shoe to the sole all round outside. Cut a sole of white paper a little smaller than the first; gum it, and fix it inside. Make a back, and sew it neatly to the shoe. Fill with scented wadding, sweetmeats, &c., according to fancy. If the articles on the tree are raffled for, and the tree is intended for grown-up girls, as sometimes happens at a Christmas party, it causes much mirth to secrete a mock wedding-ring in one of the shoes, underneath the sugar-plums or wadding. Then make known to the company that there is a ring to be found, and predict that the finder will be the first married. The lucky shoe is a very good place for it, as shoes have, in superstitious times, always been associated with supposed charms—the horse-shoe to keep away evil spirits, the old shoe for luck to be thrown after the bride, the shoes crossed at the bedside to make the owner dream of her sweetheart, &c.

46 A private view.

If the Victorians were enthusiastic in their decoration of the home, they were just as anxious for their churches to be aptly arrayed for Christmas:

> The middle aisle is a very pretty shady walk, and the pews look like so many arbours on each side of it. The pulpit itself has such clusters of ivy, holly and rosemary about it that a light fellow in our pew took occasion to say that the congregation heard the Word out of a bush, like Moses.

Once again *Cassell's Household Guide* comes to the aid of the ladies of the parish with copious instructions on the decoration of churches and school-rooms:

If there is a gallery to the church, it may be ornamented by tying garlands of evergreens close together on a rope with twine, so as to form a *cordon*. Fasten it along the front of the gallery in regular festoons, with a shield over the hollow of each festoon. A set of banners bearing the Christian attributes, Faith, Hope, Charity, Perseverance, Piety, Long-suffering, Love to God, Forbearance, Prayer, Praise, Humility, Sympathy, &c., could be very effectively used. Standard gaslights should be dressed with moderate-sized bouquets of holly and berries. The columns should be wreathed with cordons of evergreen.

The decorations of churches should be in keeping with the architecture. Rich carved work should not be touched, but blank spaces covered. A font that has not a carved cover may be enriched with a flat top, decorated with flowers in clay. The Late Pointed style of architecture, as it is called, which has columns with shafts marked by flutes, large windows near together, and screen-work, is best ornamented with shields, monograms, and small ornaments frequently placed. The columns should not be wreathed. Plain columns may have garlands of flowers round the capitals and base, with or without wreaths all down them. The mere circle round the capitals of columns and the display of texts on the bare walls, suits the heavy Norman architecture best. The Early Pointed style is very well decorated with geometrical combinations of ornament.

To obtain the shape of a shield, first draw a heart on paper, making it rather long for the width, afterwards rule a straight line across the top, marking above the semicircles. The shield shape is thus constructed. Shields may be suspended by coloured ribbon below the capitals of columns, the capitals having wreaths of evergreen round them.

The illustration shows (p. 65) the decoration of church pillars. The two styles shown in A and B should not be mixed in one church. A is decorated with a double wreath at the top, and a shield hung on the column by means of ribbon or coloured tape. B is an evergreen cordon. If the decoration B is used, then between the arches shields may be placed in the manner shown, suspended by a ribbon with a triple bow. A nail must be fixed in the wall, to which a bunch of evergreens can be tied. The shield is hung over this by the ribbon from a second nail higher up, and the ribbon passed behind the bouquet of evergreens.

To decorate a schoolroom or hall for Christmas, make a cordon of evergreens on a rope. Fix nails close to the ceiling at regular intervals, and suspend the cordon in festoons. Make hoops of crinoline cane, which cost a halfpenny each, as large as a family tea-tray. Hang these on the walls at intervals, after they have been covered with evergreens. Cut a number of pieces of scarlet, blue, and yellow silk or glazed calico, like banner hand-screens. Take a sheet of gold paper, pencil letters on the back, and cut them out. With these form

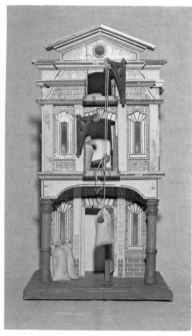

1. A superbly dressed doll by the French maker, Jumeau, 1890.

2. A mechanical knitting cat, c. 1880.

3. A model of a corn merchant's warehouse, c. 1890.

4. An enamelled tin model of a Victoria carriage designed to be pulled along the floor, c. 1885.

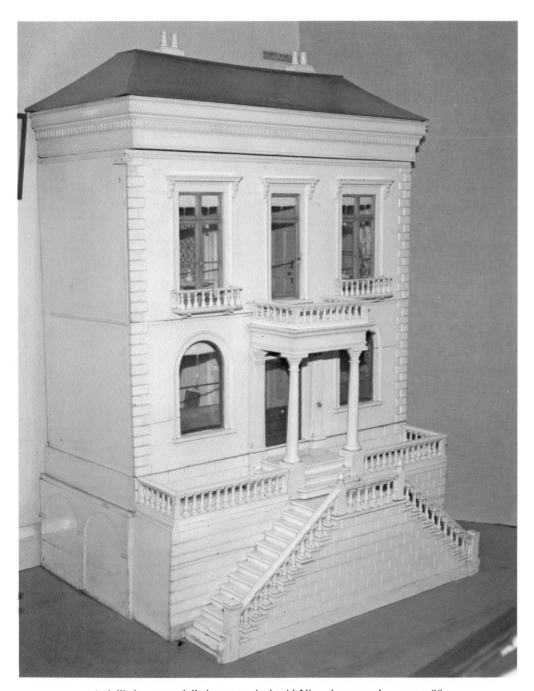

5. A doll's house modelled on a typical mid-Victorian town house, c. 1860.

6. The children hold their Christmas presents while the porter wrestles with the family pets, c. 1880.

7 & 8. Two typical mid-Victorian Christmas cards with pierced paper surrounds.

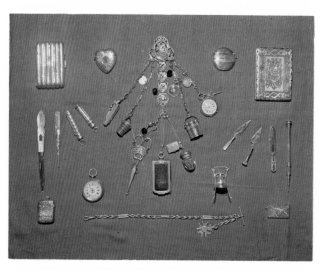

9. A collection of silver objects that could have been bought from most jewellers and silversmiths in the Victorian period, making perfect Christmas presents.

10. A Victorian Christmas plate, c. 1875.

11. Surprisingly few Victorian Christmas cards made use of religious subjects.

13 & 14. Two cards which illustrate one of the favourite preoccupations of Victorian artists—children and animals.

Compliments of the Season

12. 'Goodwill to all men' interpreted with a certain amount of licence by a Victorian Christmas card artist.

A HAPPY CHRISTMAS TO YOU

15. An amateur-designed Christmas card of the 1860s, showing a curious sense of humour.

A Happy Christmas.

16. The Holly Cart—an illustration from one of the many Christmas supplements to magazines which were published in the late nineteenth century.

17. A Christmas carol.

18. The season's greetings—after mattins in the country churchyard.

19. Guests arrive for Christmas in the country.

A   B

The Victorians were particularly conscious of the importance of decorating the church as well as the home. Here two ladies put holly round the pulpit (**48**) (*c.* 1890), and a little girl brings her contribution to 'the vicar's cluster', (**49**), (1870).

48

49

sentences on the banners, such as 'A Merry Christmas,' 'Welcome,' 'Be Merry and Wise,' 'Peace and Good Will.' Cut fringe from the gold paper and edge the banners. Cut cane the length of the top, gum the top of the banner over the cane, and fix pink tape ends to hang it from the wall, as the shields are hung in Fig. 1. A banner is to be placed in the centre of each hoop. The cordon of flowers round the top of the wall will be improved by a few crimson and pink paper flowers, sewn on at intervals. To make these, fold in strips a sheet of tissue paper; trace a tea-saucer on it, and cut out the round from the doubled paper. Crimp the paper with a reader's knife. About six rounds, sewn together in the centre at the back and pinched into shape, make the rose. At the principal end of the room let the cordon from the ceiling form a double festoon, with white calico between the loops, on which an appropriate sentence or motto is inscribed.

Pieces of crinoline cane, or lath, tied across and covered with evergreen bound on with twine, make good crosses for church decoration.

To make texts of cut-out letters, paper, silk, cloth, or velvet may be used. The initial letter of every word may be large and of one colour, the other letters small and black, or of another colour. Or alternate colours may be used for the words. Wall-paper offers a good ground for texts. Red cloth paper, as a ground, may have on it blue, gold, and black letters. Blue cloth paper—gold, scarlet, green, and silver letters. Pale green—scarlet, gold, and violet letters. Violet—red, gold, silver, and black. Suitable papers and substances for text grounds are morocco paper, paper imitating straw plait, fancy wood, mother-of-pearl, and papers with small gold patterns on them. These fancy papers can be had of most fancy stationers, and the wall-papers from paper-hangers. To make the crosses and circles correctly, a box of instruments is needed—one that includes a compass, a rule, and a bow-pencil. A box lid, if quite even, may be substituted for a rule. A bow-pencil can be improvised by taking a drawing-pin or a packing-needle and tying a string to it. Stick it well in the paper. Measure the distance for the size of the circle, and tie the other end of the string to the pencil. Then carry the pencil all round on the paper at the full length of the string. Drawing-pins also serve to fix texts in many parts of a church. They may be inserted all round like borders, and they do not damage woodwork, which is a recommendation for their use.

Paste all the letters to be used in forming a text at the back, and lay them on a clean newspaper. Do not put more paste than necessary. Fix on one at a time, pressing it with a clean soft rag or handkerchief—so as to absorb and remove any superfluous moisture—or a few sheets of blotting paper.

To make the paste, take three tablespoonfuls of flour, and as much powdered rosin as will lie on a shilling. Mix nicely in half a pint of water, and then stir it over the fire in a saucepan till it boils. Boil it for five minutes. Use cold.

It will not keep long. The paste-brush must be cleansed in boiling water, and wiped every time it is used.

In mediæval times the following significance was given to colour:—White was emblematical of light, purity, virginity, faith, joy, and life. Carmine red, of Christ's passion and death, of royalty, of the Holy Spirit, and of fire. Blue, of truth, constancy, piety. Dark red, of anger, war, and bloodshed. Gold and bright yellow, of the sun, of brightness, marriage, and fruitfulness. Dingy yellow, of deceit and jealousy. Green, of hope, of spring, prosperity, victory, immortality. Violet, of love, truth, humility, passion, and suffering. Black, of death, mourning, humiliation; also of the earth. Blue with gold stars, of heaven. White and red roses, of love and innocence, or love and wisdom.

Christmas Eve.

The Christmas fires brightly beam
And dance among the holly boughs,
The Christmas pudding's spicy steam
With fragrance fills the house,
While merry grows each friendly soul
Over the foaming wassail bowl.

The Christmas Fires,
ANNE P. L. FIELD

CHRISTMAS Eve in the nineteenth century was a busy time—a time for arrivals and for last-minute preparations before the day itself dawned. For children it was a time of excited anticipation. For many, at boarding schools, it was the end of the winter term and the beginning of the Christmas holidays. For the carol-singers it was a busy evening, and for Father Christmas, a busy night.

Christmas Eve was also a day for travelling. Those who were going to spend Christmas with friends or relatives travelled by train or coach. Both modes of travel were crowded and uncomfortable. Everyone brought food and drink for the journey and to present to their hosts. Everyone had more than the usual number of cases and parcels, and everyone was in a hurry. And yet, descriptions of Christmas Eve journeys were always full of merriment, and the excitement of the occasion seemed usually to outweigh the discomfort of the moment.

Nowhere in nineteenth-century literature is there a more evocative description of Christmas Eve travel than in Washington Irving's 'Old Christmas'.

In the course of a December tour in Yorkshire, I rode for a long distance in one of the public coaches, on the day preceding Christmas. The coach was

50 The Norfolk coach arrives at an inn on Christmas Eve (1846).

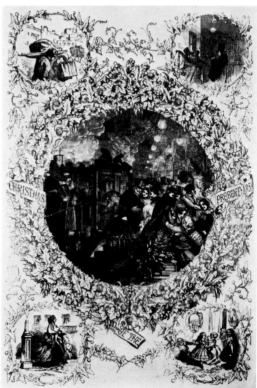

51 A Victorian railway station on Christmas Eve (1859).

52 The interior of a coaching inn on Christmas Eve, *c.* 1845. Eating, drinking and dancing are indiscriminately mixed.

53 The arrival of the Christmas train on the Eastern Counties line (1850).

54 Home for the holidays – the eldest son returns from school (1860).

55 A favourite uncle arrives for Christmas (1871).

crowded, both inside and out, with passengers, who, by their talk, seemed principally bound to the mansions of relations or friends to eat the Christmas Dinner. It was loaded also with hampers of game, and baskets and boxes of delicacies; and hares hung dangling their long ears about the coachman's box—presents from distant friends for the impending feast. I had three fine rosy-cheeked schoolboys for my fellow-passengers inside, full of the buxom health and manly spirit which I have observed in the children of this country.

They were returning home for the holidays in high glee, and promising themselves a world of enjoyment. It was delightful to hear the gigantic plans of pleasure of the little rogues, and the impracticable feats they were to perform during their six weeks' emancipation from the abhorred thraldom of books, birch and pedagogue. They were full of anticipations of the meeting with the family and the household, down to the very cat and dog; and of the joy they were to give their little sisters by the presents with which their pockets were crammed; but the meeting to which they seemed to look forward with the greatest impatience was with Bantam, which I found to be a pony, and, according to their talk, possessed of more virtues than any steed since the days of Bucephalus. . . .

Perhaps it might be owing to the pleasing serenity that reigned in my own mind, that I fancied I saw cheerfulness in every countenance throughout the journey. A stage-coach, however, carries animation always with it, and puts the world in motion as it whirls along. The horn, sounded at the entrance of a village, produces a general battle. Some hasten forth to meet friends; some with bundles and band-boxes to secure places, and in the hurry of the moment can hardly take leave of the group that accompanies them. In the meantime, the coachman has a world of small commissions to execute. Sometimes he delivers a hare or pheasant; sometimes jerks a small parcel or newspaper to the door of a public house; and sometimes, with knowing leer and words of sly import, hands to some half blushing, half laughing housemaid an odd-shaped billet-doux from some rustic admirer. . . . Resuming our route, a turn of the road brought us in sight of a neat country seat. I could just distinguish the forms of a lady and two young girls in the portico . . . I leaned out of the coach window in hopes of witnessing a happy meeting, but a grove of trees shut it from my sight.

In the evening we reached a village where I had determined to pass the night. As we drove into the great gateway of the inn, I saw on one side the light of a rousing kitchen fire beaming through a window. I entered, and admired, for the hundredth time, that picture of convenience, neatness, and broad, honest enjoyment, the kitchen of an English inn. It was of spacious dimensions, hung round with copper and tin vessels, highly polished, and decorated here and there with a Christmas green. Hams, tongues, and flitches of bacon were suspended from the ceiling; a smoke-jack made a ceaseless clanking beside the fireplace, and a clock ticked in one corner. A well scoured deal table extended along one side of the kitchen, with a cold round of beef and other hearty viands upon it over which two foaming tankards of ale seemed mounting guard.

Washington Irving may have spent the night before Christmas at an inn, but most people in the nineteenth century were by then well in the bosom of the family. As they settled down for the first night of the Christmas holiday, the voices of carol-singers, young and old, good, bad and indifferent, would have floated in from the night air.

Carol-singing was another Christmas tradition to which the Victorians gave a new lease of life. The first known collection of English carols was published in 1521 by Wynkyn de Worde, and a fragment of it remains in the Bodleian Library. Between the sixteenth and nineteenth centuries many carols were undoubtedly sung, but few were published. It was the Victorians who collected, composed and published old and new carols—

56 A visit to the grandparents on Christmas Eve (1865).

57 The ballad-monger and his family walk the streets before Christmas singing and selling Christmas carols (1847).

58 Carols outside the manor house (1859).

59 Rustic carollers – a scene in Yorkshire
(1864).

60 The family trio (1890).

some for use in church and some for home enjoyment. And, as Christmas approached, children and sometimes even adults took to the streets with their lanterns and mufflers in ever-increasing numbers in order to sing carols.

Nineteenth-century London was a musical city. During a day's walk through the metropolis one could easily have run into several groups of musicians playing on the streets. An article in *The Strand Magazine* of 1892 introduced its readers to some of the more familiar of the city's music makers. There was the lone fiddler, the blind penny-whistler and MacTosh, the Highland Piper with his boy dancer. From Italy came the Italian bagpiper, the accordion players, the organ grinders with their children and monkeys, and the street pianists. These were joined by the Indian tom-tom player, the hurdy-gurdy man, the bassoon-player, and 'old blowhard', the trumpeter. More exotic were the bellringer with his string of ten bells and the man who played the musical glasses. Then there was the one-man-band and the ballad singer with his portable harmonium, the German Band and, last but not least, the troupe of Nigger Minstrels. Add to these the shrill piping of treble voices raised in a carol and we get some idea of just how musical the Victorian city must have been in the weeks leading up to Christmas. Perhaps Scrooge's lack of enthusiasm for his carol-singer is not quite so incomprehensible as it at first appears:

> The owner of one scant young nose, gnawed and mumbled by the hungry cold as bones are gnawed by dogs, stooped down at Scrooge's keyhole to regale him with a Christmas carol: but at the first sound of
>
> > 'God rest you merry gentleman!
> > May nothing you dismay!'
>
> Scrooge seized the ruler with such energy of action, that the singer fled in terror, leaving the keyhole to the fog and even more congenial frost.

But not all carol-singers were received with such fury. It was generally the custom in nineteenth-century England to invite the wassailers into the house for a glass of punch and a mince pie. One can't help wondering how many of the Italian organ-grinder's children were sent out with their lanterns and their carol books to make their contribution to the day's earnings!

It was in the country and in the villages that Victorian artists liked to portray carol-singers—struggling against the elements, reading the words

61 Carols outside the drawing room door (1866).

62 Street musicians making the most of it (1853).

63 Could it be Father Christmas? – more likely the street band (1876).

in the feeble glow of the lantern and very probably warding off the non-singers with their snowballs and pranks. One little knot of country carol-singers provided a wistful memory for a Londoner in 1855:

As we sit in our dark and dusty chamber, made bright to-day by sprigs of holly and mistletoe (we shall increase Mrs. Scrubs our laundress' Christmas-box for her thoughtfulness), we can almost fancy that our grey hair is auburn once again, and that those rows of dusty books are the bright oak panels of our dear old country home. Our pinched-up fire expands into a capacious ingle, and that mixture of coke and slates becomes huge blocks of bituminous coal, and gnarled logs that sparkle and sputter as they are vanquished by the fire. The soot upon the dirty windowpanes crystallises, and assumes a thousand shapes of beauty, as though the frost had breathed upon it, and changed it to the pure dew which rises from Camber Vale! The hum of London streets becomes a measured harmony, and we can hear one of our countryside carols as plainly as though it were sung by the small detachment of our village choir upon which we looked the last Christmas-day we spent in the old home. Four-teen years ago, and yet we can see that group as though they stood before us in the body—Lucy Lot in one of the Squire's lady's left-off bonnets and a white boa made of lamb's tails. She has a pipe like a robin and her

> Bless you, my good gentlemen,
> May nothing you dismay,

rises clear and shrill over all competitors. [Only to think! little Lucy Lot is now the buxom wife of George Weathers, the butcher, and the proprietor of a brace of babies.]

Jenny Ryland is not half such a belle as Lucy Lot. She wears a little modest poke, as they call that rough straw bonnet. True, she has a red whittle; but her frock is a dark brown, and her gloves are of grey worsted. She sings very correctly, notwithstanding she has to shake the chorus out of her little brother Bob, who is all clothes and face. He is a very good boy, and will make a singer in time, but at present a word of three syllables chokes him. If he live to be a man——[Why he has lived to be a man—in his own opinion—and, though only nineteen last June, he has been seen walking with Mary Jessop, who lives fellow-servant with his sister at the Hall. Sister has a sweetheart, too—a widower—grocer, cheesemonger, and general dealer. I forgot to say that Bob is by trade a blacksmith.]

Overleaf: Two of the most famous carols beloved of the Victorians – 'God rest you merry, Gentlemen' (**64**), and 'Good King Wenceslas' (**65**) – all with typical illustrative headpieces (1875).

I.

God rest you, merry Gentlemen.

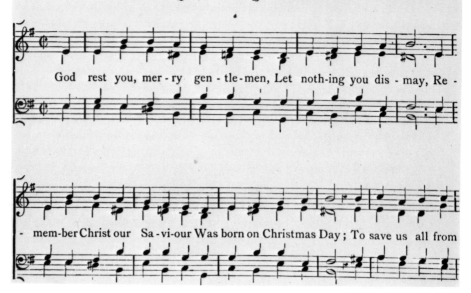

God rest you, mer-ry gen-tle-men, Let noth-ing you dis-may, Re-

-mem-ber Christ our Sa-vi-our Was born on Christmas Day; To save us all from

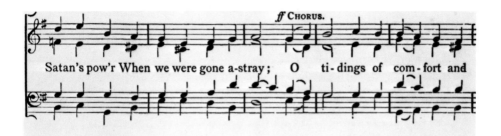

Satan's pow'r When we were gone a-stray; O ti-dings of com-fort and

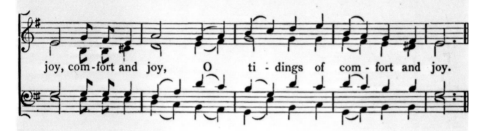

joy, com-fort and joy, O ti-dings of com-fort and joy.

2.

In Bethlehem, in Jewry,
    This blessed Babe was born,
And laid within a manger,
    Upon this blessed Morn ;
The which His Mother Mary,
    Did nothing take in scorn.
        O tidings, &c.

3.

From God our Heavenly Father,
    A blessed Angel came ;
And unto certain Shepherds,
    Brought tidings of the same :
How that in Bethlehem was born ;
    The Son of God by Name.
        O tidings, &c.

4.

" Fear not then," said the Angel,
    " Let nothing you affright,
This day is born a Saviour
    Of a pure Virgin bright,
To free all those that trust in Him
    From Satan's power and might."
        O tidings, &c.

5.

The shepherds at those tidings,
    Rejoicèd much in mind,
And left their flocks a-feeding,
    In tempest, storm, and wind :
And went to Bethlehem straightway,
    The Son of God to find.
        O tidings, &c.

6.

And when they came to Bethlehem,
    Where our dear Saviour lay,
They found Him in a manger,
    Where oxen feed on hay ;
His Mother Mary kneeling down,
    Unto the Lord did pray.
        O tidings, &c.

7.

Now to the Lord sing praises,
    All you within this place,
And with true love and brotherhood
    Each other now embrace ;
The holy tide of Christmas
    All other doth deface.
        O tidings, &c.

X. **Good King Wenceslas.**

CHORUS.

Good King Wen - ces - las look'd out, On the Feast of Ste - phen,

When the snow lay round a - bout, Deep, and crisp and e - ven:

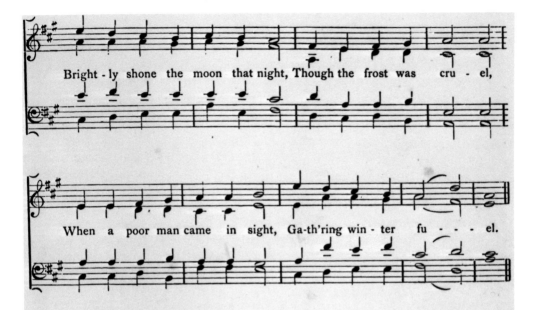

Bright - ly shone the moon that night, Though the frost was cru - el,

When a poor man came in sight, Ga-th'ring win - ter fu - - - el.

Tenor Solo.   2.
" Hither, page, and stand by me,
    If thou know'st it, telling,
Yonder peasant, who is he ?
    Where and what his dwelling?"
Treble Solo.
" Sire, he lives a good league hence,
    Underneath the mountain ;
Right against the forest fence,
    By Saint Agnes' fountain."

Tenor Solo.   3.
" Bring me flesh, and bring me wine,
    Bring me pine-logs hither :
Thou and I will see him dine,
    When we bear them thither."
Chorus.
Page and monarch forth they went,
    Forth they went together ;
Through the rude wind's wild lament
    And the bitter weather.

Treble Solo.   4.
" Sire, the night is darker now,
    And the wind blows stronger ;
Fails my heart, I know not how,
    I can go no longer."
Tenor Solo.
" Mark my footsteps, good my page ;
    Tread thou in them boldly:
Thou shalt find the winter's rage
    Freeze thy blood less coldly."

Chorus.   5.
In his master's steps he trod,
    Where the snow lay dinted ;
Heat was in the very sod
    Which the saint had printed.
Therefore, Christian men, be sure,
    Wealth or rank possessing,
Ye who now will bless the poor,
    Shall yourselves find blessing.

There is Charley Brown—his nose the colour of a blue bag. He hates the cold and gives promise of having a bad cold in the head in the morning. He may be saved by egg-hot or toast and ale in the evening, but at present his prospects are gruel. [He did have the egg-hot and the cold and gruel, and still entertains an objection to the weather when the glass falls below zero. He has done the best he could to keep himself warm by adopting the trade of a baker.]

Jack Bray is the tall one of the party. He is only thirteen, but he has a voice like an ophicleide—he is the awkwardest lad in the village—he don't walk, he rolls along, and it is a matter of doubt whether he affects the right-hand ditch or the left-hand ditch. His ultimate destination is certainly one of them. [And Jack Bray has been for a soldier and fought nobly at Alma and Inkerman. He was at the storming of the Redan, where he lost an arm, and has been sent home invalided. He tells stirring stories of his comrades, who, reckless of all but victory, faced dangers and death, knowing that their chances of escape were small indeed. And often, Jack says, as they sat round their scanty fires they have spoken of home and those they left behind to fight the battles of life alone, and have wondered, when the next Christmas time came round, if any would make their poor homes merry for the sake of those who were away doing their country's work. And Jack says they were hopeful—all hopeful; and he has promised to write to them when Christmas time is passed. Let him have a good story to tell countrymen.]

Where are the singers gone? Where the song? Where the old home? Gone! But we have been made happy thinking of the Christmas time.

(M. L.)

The last and most important visitor to arrive on Christmas Eve was Father Christmas or Santa Claus.

The character of the mid-Victorian Father Christmas was a curious conglomeration of legend and reality, fact and fiction that had its roots in the fourth century A.D. St Nicholas was Bishop of Myra in Asia Minor in that century and was believed to have been immensely rich. His chief delight in life was to shed himself of his riches whenever a deserving case presented itself. So it was that three sisters whose father was too poor to give them dowries awoke one morning to find three bags of gold which St Nicholas had thrown in through the window in the night. These three bags of gold have become stylized as the three golden balls of the pawnbroker whose patron St Nicholas is.

Another recipient of the episcopal bounty found that her bag of gold had landed in a stocking drying in front of the fire. The athletic bishop had thrown it down the chimney! Ever since then girls and boys throughout the Christian world have hung up their stockings or put out their shoes either on St Nicholas' Day, 6 December, or on Christmas Eve.

But to the Victorians Father Christmas was more than just St Nicholas. He was also closely related to the early nineteenth-century 'Spirit of Christmas', who was seldom depicted without a glass in his hand. This jovial figure was the one most often seen in Victorian Christmas pictures. He was shown as the founder of the Christmas Feast, the purveyor of jollity as well as the children's present-giver. Half pagan and half Christian, he inspired awe as well as love. But in the latter half of the century he became less associated with carousing and more akin to his European counter-

66 The woodman returns home on Christmas Eve (1865).

67 The cottager returns from the market on Christmas Eve (*c.* 1845).

68 Christmas Eve for the less fortunate meant tramping the city streets without much expectation of joy on the morrow (1851).

Hang up the baby's stocking! Be sure you don't forget! The dear little dimpled darling, she never saw Christmas yet! But I've told her all about it, and she opened her big blue eyes; and I'm sure she understood it—she looked so funny and wise. ∴ Dear, what a tiny stocking! It doesn't take much to hold such little pink toes as baby's away from the frost and cold. But then, for the baby's Christmas, it will never do at all. Why! Santa wouldn't be looking for anything half so small. ∴ I know what will do for the baby. I've thought of the very best plan. I'll borrow a stocking of Grandma's, the longest that ever I can. And you'll hang it by mine, dear mother, right here in the corner, so! And leave a letter to Santa, and fasten it on to the toe. ∴ Write—this is the baby's stocking, that hangs in the corner here. You never have seen her, Santa, for she only came this year. But she's just the blessed'st baby. And now before you go, just cram her stocking with goodies, from the top clean down to the toe!

69 'Hang up the baby's stocking!' – a splendid piece of Victorian typography.

70 'Santa Claus' (from *The Strand Magazine*, 1891) – a curiously late appearance in England of the Christkind.

parts—the German Christkind, the Scandinavian St Lucy and the Dutch-American Santa Claus. Although, unlike some of them, he was never accompanied by an avenging angel ready to chastise naughty children. Largely through the American influence he became a jolly, fat, red-habited man who arrived in a sleigh drawn by reindeer. This was the figure that Clement Clark Moore partly created and certainly immortalized when in 1822 he wrote his poem 'A Visit from St Nicholas'.

'Twas the night before Christmas, when all through the house
Not a creature was stirring, not even a mouse;
The stockings were hung by the chimney with care,
In hopes that St. Nicholas soon would be there;
The children were nestled all snug in their beds,
While visions of sugar-plums danced through their heads;
And mamma in her kerchief, and I in my cap,
Had just settled our brains for a long winter's nap,—
When out on the lawn there arose such a clatter,
I sprang from my bed to see what was the matter.
Away to the window I flew like a flash,
Tore open the shutters and threw up the sash.
The moon, on the breast of the new-fallen snow,
Gave a lustre of midday to objects below;
When what to my wondering eyes should appear,
But a miniature sleigh and eight tiny reindeer,
With a little old driver, so lively and quick
I knew in a moment it must be St. Nick.
More rapid than eagles his coursers they came,
And he whistled and shouted and called them by name:
'Now, Dasher! now, Dancer! now, Prancer and Vixen!
On, Comet! on, Cupid! on, Donder and Blitzen!
To the top of the porch, to the top of the wall!
Now, dash away, dash away, dash away all!'
As dry leaves that before the wild hurricane fly,
When they meet with an obstacle, mount to the sky,
So, up to the house-top the coursers they flew,
With a sleigh full of toys,—and St. Nicholas too.
And then in a twinkling I heard on the roof
The prancing and pawing of each little hoof,
As I drew in my head and was turning around,
Down the chimney St. Nicholas came with a bound.
He was dressed all in fur from his head to his foot,

And his clothes were all tarnished with ashes and soot;
A bundle of toys he had flung on his back,
And he looked like a pedler just opening his pack.
His eyes how they twinkled! his dimples how merry!
His cheeks were like roses, his nose like a cherry;
His droll little mouth was drawn up like a bow,
And the beard on his chin was as white as the snow.
The stump of a pipe he held tight in his teeth,
And the smoke it encircled his head like a wreath.
He had a broad face, and a little round belly
That shook, when he laughed, like a bowl full of jelly.
He was chubby and plump,—a right jolly old elf—
And I laughed when I saw him, in spite of myself.
A wink of his eye and a twist of his head
Soon gave me to know I had nothing to dread.
He spoke not a word, but went straight to his work,
And filled all the stockings; then turned with a jerk,
And laying his finger aside of his nose,
And giving a nod, up the chimney he rose.
He sprang to his sleigh, to his team gave a whistle,
And away they all flew like the down of a thistle;
But I heard him exclaim, ere he drove out of sight:
'Happy Christmas to all, and to all a goodnight!'

It was a happy piece of writing describing a character totally different to the ascetic saint on his grey horse. And quite quickly children on both sides of the Atlantic became familiar with Clement Moore's description of 'St Nick'. But neither the Americans nor the English were able to agree with Moore about the costume. From about 1850 in America artists have portrayed Santa Claus in a red suit with a matching cap, whereas in England Father Christmas has been depicted in a red habit with hood. Like the white beard, however, the sleigh and reindeer achieved universal recognition. Paul Howard in 'Christmas in America' describes the American Santa Claus with boundless enthusiasm:

An old English legend was transplanted many years ago on the shores of America, that took root and flourished with wonderful luxuriance, considering it was not indigenous to the country. Probably it was taken over to New York by one of the primitive Knickerbockers, or it might have clung to some of the drowsy burgomasters who had forsaken the pictorial tiles of dear old

71   **72**

73

JOLLY OLD CHRISTMAS.

71 The Christmas Spirit as seen by the early Victorians was a very different figure from the white-bearded, red-habited character who came into prominence towards the end of the nineteenth century (1843).

72 'What, Father Christmas! here again? with Yule log on your back' (1848).

73 'Jolly Old Christmas' (1843).

74 'Christmas for ever!' (1857).

75 'King Cheer' – one of the titles of the Spirit of Christmas (1864).

76 Father Christmas – an impromptu performance
by one of the family (1866).

77 The Spirit of Christmas, in jovial mood, invites the onlooker to share the feast (1845).

78 'Here comes Santa Claus!' (1891).

Amsterdam about the time of Peter de Laar, or Il Bombaccia, as the Italians call him, got into disgrace in Rome. However this may be, certain it is that Santa Claus, or St. Nicholas, the kind Patron-saint of the Juveniles, makes his annual appearance on Christmas Eve, for the purpose of dispensing gifts to all good children. This festive elf is supposed to be a queer little creature that descends the chimney, viewlessly, in the deep hours of night, laden with gifts and presents, which he bestows with no sparing hand, reserving to himself a supernatural discrimination that he seems to exercise with every satisfaction. Before going to bed the children hang their newest stockings near the chimney, or pin them to the curtains of the bed. Midnight finds a world of hosiery waiting for favours; and the only wonder is that a single Santa Claus can get around among them all. The story goes that he never misses one, provided it belongs to a deserving youngster, and morning is sure to bring no reproach that the Christmas Wizard has not nobly performed his wondrous duties. We need scarcely enlighten the reader as to who the real Santa Claus is. Every indulgent parent contributes to the pleasing deception, though the juveniles are strong in their faith of their generous holiday patron.

So there he is, the Victorian Father Christmas or Santa Claus, in his 'world of hosiery', silently dispensing gifts before climbing up the chimney again to disappear into the night sky—or, if Mr Howard is to be believed, before creeping along the corridor to bed. Whichever way he left, Father Christmas was the last visitor to the Victorian household on Christmas Eve. With his departure the whole family slept, no doubt with visions of the day to come.

Christmas Morning.

---◆---

He comes—the brave old Christmas!
His sturdy steps I hear;
We will give him a hearty welcome,
For he comes but once a year!

> *Welcome to Christmas,*
> MARY HOWITT

---◆---

CHRISTMAS morning in the early Victorian period seemed often to dawn bright, snow-covered and crisp as any of the Christmas cards sent or received over the previous month. Winters in the 1830s and 1840s were well remembered for their harshness. There were numerous incidents of stage coaches being stranded and villages being cut off by the snow. But as the century progressed such winters became fewer and the white Christmas became the exception rather than the rule. Nevertheless artists like Birket Foster and the designers of Christmas cards strenuously maintained the illusion that snow was an invariable ingredient of the Christmas scene, and the public demanded this romantic image.

Children would awake early on Christmas morning to find that Father Christmas had filled their stockings with sweets, toys and fruit. When they could no longer contain their excitement they peeped into their parents' room to wish them a 'Happy Christmas'. Then, taken back to the night nursery, they were dressed and their hair was brushed before breakfast.

And so, filled with anticipation of the excitements to come, perhaps with dreams of plum pudding at lunch, the Victorian family set out through the snow for church on Christmas morning to hear the parson's Christmas sermon, to say the familiar Christmas prayers and to sing the traditional Christmas carols. For most middle-class Victorians, mattins on Christmas morning was one of the focal points of the day. It was only after duty done that the presents and the midday meal could be enjoyed. Among the work-

97

ing classes, however, religious observation was by no means so widespread. Tradesmen still traded—bakers kept their ovens alight to cook the local families' Christmas geese and poulterers stayed open in the hope of selling just one more turkey.

It was the last prize turkey that Scrooge bought for the Cratchits on that glorious morning that witnessed his transformation:

> Running to the window, he opened it, and put out his head. No fog, no mist; clear, bright, jovial, stirring, cold; cold, piping for the blood to dance to; golden sunlight; heavenly sky; sweet fresh air; merry bells. Oh, glorious. Glorious!
>
> 'What's to-day?' cried Scrooge, calling downward to a boy in Sunday clothes, who perhaps had loitered in to look about him.
>
> 'Eh?' returned the boy, with all his might of wonder.
>
> 'What's to-day, my fine fellow?' said Scrooge.
>
> 'To-day!' replied the boy. 'Why, Christmas Day.'
>
> 'It's Christmas Day!' said Scrooge to himself. 'I haven't missed it. The Spirits have done it all in one night. They can do anything they like. Of course they can. Of course they can. Hallo, my fine fellow!'
>
> 'Hallo!' returned the boy.
>
> 'Do you know the Poulterer's, in the next street but one, at the corner?' Scrooge inquired.
>
> 'I should hope I did,' replied the lad.
>
> 'An intelligent boy!' said Scrooge. 'A remarkable boy! Do you know whether they've sold the prize Turkey that was hanging up there? Not the little prize Turkey: the big one?'
>
> 'What the one as big as me?' returned the boy.
>
> 'What a delightful boy!' said Scrooge. 'It's a pleasure to talk to him. Yes, my buck!'
>
> 'It's hanging there now,' replied the boy.
>
> 'Is it?' said Scrooge. 'Go and buy it.'
>
> 'Walk-er!' exclaimed the boy.
>
> 'No, no,' said Scrooge, 'I am in earnest. Go and buy it, and tell 'em to bring it here, that I may give them the direction where to take it. Come back with the man, and I'll give you a shilling. Come back with him in less than five minutes, and I'll give you half-a crown!'
>
> The boy was off like a shot. He must have had a steady hand at a trigger who could have got a shot off half so fast.
>
> 'I'll send it to Bob Cratchit's!' whispered Scrooge, rubbing his hands, and splitting with a laugh. 'He shan't know who sends it. It's twice the size of Tiny Tim. Joe Miller never made such a joke as sending it to Bob's will be!'

79 'A Happy Christmas to Papa and Mamma.' (1874).

80 Even on Christmas Day the postman arrived (*c.* 1870).

81 'The Birds' Christmas' – a typical piece of Victorian sentimentality (*c.* 1865).

82

83

Christmas wasn't Christmas without snow and although white Christmases were never so common as Victorian artists liked to imagine, few Christmas illustrations lacked a fine white covering. The child's first snowball (**82**), (*c.* 1860), 'Boys will be boys' (**83**) (1850) and 'Gathering as it goes'. (**84**) (1855).

84

The hand in which he wrote the address was not a steady one, but write it he did, somehow, and went down stairs to open the street door, ready for the coming of the poulterer's man. As he stood there, waiting his arrival, the knocker caught his eye.

'I shall love it, as long as I live!' cried Scrooge, patting it with his hand. 'I scarcely ever looked at it before. What an honest expression it has in its face! It's a wonderful knocker!—Here's the Turkey. Hallo! Whoop! How are you! Merry Christmas!'

It *was* a Turkey! He could never had stood upon his legs, that bird. He would have snapped 'em short off in a minute, like sticks of sealing-wax.

'Why, it's impossible to carry that to Camden Town,' said Scrooge. 'You must have a cab.'

The chuckle with which he said this, and the chuckle with which he paid for the turkey, and the chuckle with which he paid for the cab, and the chuckle with which he recompensed the boy, were only to be exceeded by the chuckle with which he sat down breathless in his chair again, and chuckled till he cried.

Shaving was not an easy task, for his hand continued to shake very much; and shaving requires attention, even when you don't dance while you are at it. But if he had cut the end of his nose off, he would have put a piece of sticking-plaster over it, and been quite satisfied.

He dressed himself 'all in his best', and at last got out into the streets. The people were by this time pouring forth, as he had seen them with the Ghost of Christmas Present; and walking with his hands behind him, Scrooge regarded everyone with a delighted smile. He looked so irresistibly pleasant, in a word, that three or four good-humoured fellows said, 'Good morning, Sir! A Merry Christmas to you!' And Scrooge said often afterwards, that of all the blithe sounds he had ever heard, those were the blithest in his ears.

For another glimpse of a Christmas morning later in the century, we can turn again to George R. Sims:

It is Christmas morning. London does not rise so early as usual today, and it is well on towards ten o'clock before there is any considerable movement. Then people who are going to spend the day with friends in the suburbs or at some little distance, begin to make their way to the railway stations. Here are youths and maidens hastening by themselves, here an aged man and woman making their way slowly, here are family parties, papa and mama, and olive branches innumerable. Almost without exception each bears a brown paper parcel. It is the Christmas gift, the little present that is usually

85 A timely reminder that Christmas wasn't all fun for certain sections of Victorian society. A poor seamstress in her garret on Christmas morning (1877).

86 The village choir rehearses the Christmas Anthem (1871).

taken to the hosts by the visitors—to Uncle John, to Aunt Mary, to the cousins, to grandmama and grandpapa.

All the morning long the little stream of parcel-bearers going out to spend the day with relatives and friends continues, but towards eleven it is joined by another crowd, a crowd that carries a church service instead of a paper parcel, a crowd that is spending Christmas in its own homes. The church bells are ringing merrily. When they cease there is a noticeable thinning of the stream of pedestrians. The trains on the local lines have ceased running until after Divine service, and now there are only the travellers who are taking 'bus and tram and cab to their destinations. The private carriages, the hired broughams, will not start with the little family parties outward bound until later in the day.

And with the end of Christmas Day mattins the congregations poured out of churches in town and country, shook the vicars' hands and wished each other 'Happy Christmas' before hurrying home for the warmth of the family circle. Christmas was a time for traditions for the Victorians. Not only were there national traditions, but also family ones. Whereas in the early part of the century it was customary for dinner to be taken at the eighteenth-century hour of four o'clock, it became increasingly common as the century progressed for the main meal of Christmas Day to be put forward to half-past one or back to half-past seven in the evening. The exact timing of this meal—lunch or dinner—was dictated, not only by class, but also by the absence or presence of children. So while some families opened their presents and then sat down to a light lunch to be followed by a gargantuan dinner, others enjoyed their main meal at lunch time and finished the evening with a modest supper.

Whatever the size of the midday meal, there can have been few Victorian Christmas trees that had not been stripped of their presents well before it began. Family traditions about the correct hour for opening Christmas presents were then, as now, dictated by the least patient of its members. And so, after the presents were surprises no more, amid the shrieks of delight, the rustle of paper and the whirring of clockwork toys, someone would announce that the meal was ready and the family would go through to the dining-room.

87 A Christmas morning present for the vicar (1874).

Overleaf: For the Victorian family Christmas morning meant mattins at church, the focal point of the day's activities. The family sets out for church (**88**); Christmas hymns, perhaps 'Hark the Herald angels sing' (**89**) and (**90**); the Christmas sermon (**91**).

90

91

92 Fetching home the Christmas goose. Bakers kept their ovens alight on Christmas Day to cook geese for the poorer families (1848).

Overleaf: The moment arrives – the children gather excitedly around the Christmas tree as the candles are lit and the presents opened (**93**) and (**94**).

93

94

Christmas Dinner.

Old Christmas is come for to keep open house;
He scorns to be guilty of starving a mouse:
Then come, boys, and welcome, for diet the chief,
Plum-pudding, goose, capon, minc'd pies, and roast beef.

REPRODUCED in so many Victorian books about Christmas fare, that Restoration ballad seems to echo perfectly our nineteenth-century ancestors' view of what the gastronomic side of Christmas involved. Whether eaten at midday or in the evening, the Christmas dinner was a meal to remember throughout the next year and to anticipate with pleasure. Preparations for the feast had been started weeks before with the ordering of the food and the arrangement of the menu as well as the cooking of pies and sweetmeats. The illustrations and articles in this section show the Victorians preparing as well as enjoying their Christmas dinner.

When Queen Victoria came to the throne in 1837 traditional Christmas fare in England was roast beef in the North and goose in the South, and this remained the case for several years:

... You might have thought a goose the rarest of all birds; a feathered pheno-menon, to which a black swan was a matter of course; and in truth, it was something like it in that house. Mrs. Cratchit made the gravy (ready before-hand in a little saucepan) hissing hot; Master Peter mashed the potatoes with incredible vigor; Miss Belinda sweetened up the apple-sauce; Martha dusted the hot plates; Bob took Tiny Tim beside him in a tiny corner, at the table; the two young Cratchits set chairs for everybody, not forgetting themselves, and mounting guard upon their posts, crammed spoons into their mouths, lest they should shriek for goose before their turn came to be helped. At last the dishes were set on, and grace was said. It was succeeded by a breathless pause, as Mrs. Cratchit, looking slowly all along the carving knife, prepared to plunge it in the breast; but when she did, and when the long-expected gush

95 Poulterer's shop, Holborn Hill, London (1845).

96 A grocer's shop at Christmas thronged with customers in search of those final, crucial ingredients for the Christmas table (1852).

97 Newgate Market on Christmas Eve – the busiest day of the year
(1845).

98 Leadenhall Market on Christmas Eve – last-minute shoppers could
still find poultry and game (1845).

99 Buying the Christmas goose (1882).

100 'Christmas Joints' – the butcher's boy makes his last delivery (1851).

101 'Compliments of the season' – the Christmas hampers arrive (1846).

of stuffing issued forth, one murmur of delight arose all around the board, and even Tiny Tim, excited by the two young Cratchits, beat on the table with the handle of his knife, and feebly cried hurrah!

There never was such a goose. Bob said he didn't believe there ever was such a goose cooked. Its tenderness and flavor, size and cheapness, were the themes of universal admiration. Eked out by the apple-sauce and mashed potatoes, it was a sufficient dinner for the whole family; indeed, as Mrs. Cratchit said with great delight (surveying one small atom of a bone on the dish), they hadn't ate it all at last! Yet every one had had enough, and the youngest Cratchits in particular were steeped in sage and onion to the eye-brows!

Bob Crachit's salary was fifteen shillings a week. How could he afford a goose of such magnificence? The answer lies in one of the great Victorian working-class institutions—The Goose Club. Even the lowest paid worker could enjoy a goose at Christmas with his family by contributing to his local Goose Club a small part of his week's wages throughout the year. Some Goose Clubs also raffled geese and bottles of wine or port. The fact

that they were often run from the local public houses brought these
excellent institutions in for a lot of criticism from temperance quarters:

With right good will I take my pen a story to declare,
To tell you how the luckless dupes of publicans do fare.
I'll tell you of some Christmas geese—such fowl in cities thrive—
Not only were they roasted well, but roasted all alive!

You need not frown, and lift your brows, and look so very keen,
For, haply, you may prove to be among the geese I mean.
But to my tale:—There stands hard by—to mar the public peace—
A liquor den for tempting men, that's called the 'Golden Fleece'.

Fillpot, the landlord's on the watch, and well he knows his trade;
A red-faced, freely-spoken man, who has a fortune made.
Some time ago he sat alone, pondering o'er his gold,
And thinking customers were few, considering what he sold.

Thought he—(and here he raised his head, and gave a knowing smile,
Then gravely mused a moment more, and smoked his pipe the while);
Thought he, 'I have a happy plan, that customers will bring:
A "Goose" Club, if well managed, will be just the very thing.'

Then blithely starting from his chair—'Give *me* the fools!' he cries,
'And I will sit me down content; *you're welcome* to the wise!'
To work he went with haste, and soon he got his list in print
On gaudy paper, printed large, in every showy tint.

'I can afford to give a "goose" by way of prize,' said he,
'For every foolish customer will be a goose to me.'
So shrewdly did he calculate, his plan could hardly fail;
Nine-tenths of all his prizes were a glass of gin or ale.

Besides the profit thus obtained, full well sly Fillpot knew
That most who brought a shilling there would spend another too.
Among his printed prizes were a few to catch the eye
(Adroitly in his window placed) to tempt each passer-by.

'A set of china, blue and gold; a turkey, wondrous fine;
A good fat goose; a pound of tea; a keg of foreign wine,'
A glass of gin or brandy formed a part of every prize:
Thus oft 'mid pleasure's pleasant flowers a stinging serpent lies.

'Twas strange to see, in little time, what sudden change was made;
The public-house soon carried on a brisk and growing trade.
The Goose Club was a thriving plot; the landlord sure to win;
The customers, with shillings bright, came quickly pouring in.

And thus the crafty publican, for his own private use,
By holding out his pleasant baits, contrived to catch his 'goose'.
The members who had tickets bought admired the prize-display;
But little did the green-horns think the price they had to pay.

Day after day, night after night, there came a motley throng.
To spend and drink, and laugh and talk, and hear a jovial song.
See Fillpot now, in merry vein; his Goose Club is a thing
To make a noise, to fill his house, and ready money bring.

He jokes and laughs, and looking round, with cunning in his eyes,
Tells each in turn that he is sure to get the highest prize.
And thus the wily publican, without the least excuse,
Deceives and leads astray, and then begins to pluck his 'goose'.

Well pleased are Fillpot's customers to find him frank and free;
The more they drink, the more they spend, the happier man is he.
The tap-room company indulge at night in noise and rout,
And wretched objects they appear when Fillpot turns them out.

Who's this that brandishes his stick? his reason all but gone!
And stretching out his doubled fist declares he cares for none!
And who is this—in bonds indeed!—and yet in glee he raves!—
'England for ever!—Britons, boys, are never, never slaves!'

Fillpot enjoys his ready joke, and while they shout and bawl,
'My Christmas geese are still,' thought he, 'the greatest geese of all!'
And thus the wily publican, with conscience all obtuse,
Sits down well pleased to smoke his pipe and gaily roast his goose.

The Drawing Day is come, the throng look on with anxious eyes;
But Fillpot's son, who tickets took, has got the highest prize.
And even he who won the goose was victimised by theft—
The head and neck, when he got home, was all that he had left.

And now the smiling landlord comes: he thinks it fair and due
That every one who's won a prize should spend a trifle too.

'Agreed! agreed!' some shout aloud, a merry night they make,
And spend and drink, and rave and tear, for dear old Fillpot's sake.

Tom Bates was once a workman good: in sad and evil hour
He joined the 'Goose' Club, and, alas! was soon in Fillpot's power.
In Fillpot's house he spends his all, and runs awhile in debt,
For he that will a drunkard be must soon in trouble get.

Unhappy Bates! at evening hour he hears the tap-room brawl,
And, mingling with the company, he slinks behind them all.
But wary Fillpot finds him out; looks at his unpaid score;
Secures his hat and ragged coat, and kicks him from his door.

And thus that fox, the publican, who plays at fast and loose,
Devours the flesh and picks the bones of his deluded goose.
My tale is told—I seek to give offence to none alive;
But Goose Clubs do more harm than good, and ought not to survive.

Ye landlords all, my parting wish is that you soon may find
Some nobler course to win your wealth, some better trade to mind!
Then when you close your house at night, you'll rest with heart content,
To think that none who've dealt with you are worse for what they've spent.

Just as the French left their *pommes de terre boulangère* for the baker to cook in his oven when he wasn't baking bread, so Bob Cratchit and many of his kind took their Christmas geese to the baker to be cooked, then returned home with the finished article to find the whole family waiting round the table with knives and forks at the ready. Middle-class families, however, would expect to cook their own Christmas lunch and might well have turned to Mr Buckmaster's excellent little cookery book entitled succinctly *Buckmaster's Cookery* for directions on how to cook a goose:

ROAST GOOSE.

Ingredients.

A Goose.   Duck or Chestnut stuffing.

A goose weighing six or eight pounds is to be preferred. **1.** Pick, draw, singe and wipe. **2.** Stuff it with stuffing as for roast duck or chestnut stuffing. **3.** Sprinkle with a little salt. **4.** Baste frequently. **5.** Skim off all the fat, strain the gravy over the goose, or serve separately in a sauce-boat.

Precautions.—It is essential that the goose should be young, and roasted before a good fire, but not a fierce one. Try the pinion, and if the lower part of the beak breaks easily the goose or duck is young.

The other main ingredient of the Victorian Christmas feast was the plum pudding—the one dish that symbolizes the Victorian Christmas more than any other:

But now, the plates being changed by Miss Belinda, Mrs. Cratchit left the room alone—too nervous to bear witnesses—to take the pudding up, and bring it in.

Suppose it should not be done enough! Suppose it should break in turning out! Suppose somebody should have got over the wall of the backyard, and stolen it, while they were merry with the goose; a supposition at which the two young Cratchits became livid! All sorts of horrors were supposed.

Hallo! A great deal of steam! The pudding was out of the copper. A smell like a washing-day! That was the cloth. A smell like an eating-house and a pastry cook's next door to each other, with a laundress next door to that! That was the pudding. In half a minute Mrs. Cratchit entered, flushed, but smiling proudly, with the pudding like a speckled cannon-ball, so hard and firm, blazing in half of half-a-quartern of ignited brandy, and bedight with Christmas holly stuck into the top.

Oh, a wonderful pudding! Bob Cratchit said, and calmly too, that he regarded it as the greatest success achieved by Mrs. Cratchit since their marriage. Mrs. Cratchit said that now the weight was off her mind, she would confess she had had her doubts about the quantity of flour. Everybody had something to say about it, but nobody said or thought it was at all a small pudding for so large a family. It would have been flat heresy to do so. Any Cratchit would have blushed to hint at such a thing.

Although plum pudding in the past had been made with plums (amongst other things), raisins and currants supplanted them well before the nineteenth century so that one definition of the Victorian plum pudding was 'a pudding without plums'.

Victorians upheld many of the traditions surrounding the 'speckled cannonball'. The pudding was stirred by every member of the family from East to West in honour of the Three Kings. On board ship at Christmas time it was first stirred by the senior officer. Silver charms and threepenny pieces were hidden in it during the cooking and those who would never

102 The Goose Club – the poorer classes would put money aside throughout the
year in order to be able to afford their Christmas goose (1853).

103 No Christmas lunch or dinner was complete without the Christmas pudding.
Chaos abounds as the children help to stir the pudding (1848).

104 A Christmas pudding for the lighthouse keeper (1891).

105 Christmas dinner at a prosperous Victorian household (*c.* 1890).

have dreamt of eating *flambé* dishes would have been severely disappointed if the plum pudding had not been served blazing with its garnish of holly. Victorian recipes for plum pudding are legion. There are recipes for vegetarian puddings and monster puddings, and one, used by the Queen's chef, was sufficient to make 150 small puddings for distribution to the household staff. The ingredients are fairly overpowering:

> 60 lbs. flour, 30 lbs. Lisbon sugar, 40 lbs. currants,
> 40 lbs. raisins (seeded and chopped), 30 lbs. candied peel,
> 50 lbs. chopped beef suet, 4 gallons strong ale, 150 eggs,
> 1 lb. mixed spice, 1 bottle of rum, 1 bottle of brandy.

One can almost hear the disapproval of the temperance workers. Their recipe for plum pudding was presented in rhyme by Mrs H. Beaven:

RECIPE FOR A RICH TEETOTAL PUDDING.

2 lbs. of suet-beef, quite fresh, and you must chop it fine;
1 lb. of raisins you must stone (on stones you could not dine);
1 lb. of bright sultanas pick, and in the bowl you'll mix
1 lb. of currants clean and dry, all free from grit or sticks.
¼ lb. of peel comes next, the *mixed* peel is not dear—
Orange and lemon, citron chips, this season's, fresh and clear;
3 ozs. next of almonds chop, the bitter ones please use;
1 lb. of sugar you require, the Demerara choose.
1½ lbs. of flour come next, let it be dry and sound;
1 lb of bread crumbs follows suit; be sure they're finely ground.
9 eggs next take and whisk them well, one nutmeg, only, add;
(To make things 'nice' with too much spice, in every way is bad).
Then take of salt a teaspoonful, stirred in with careful hand,
A pint of milk instead of beer, and you've a pudding grand!

Everyone was catered for. All Victorians could eat plum pudding. Mrs Beeton gave a recipe for 'fruitarian' plum pudding to suit vegetarians, and Eliza Acton, in *Modern Cookery for Private Families*, even had one for impecunious vegetarians:

VEGETABLE PLUM PUDDING.

(Cheap and good.)

Mix well together one pound of smoothly-mashed potatoes, half a pound of carrots boiled quite tender, and beaten to a paste, one pound of flour, one of currants, and one of raisins (full weight after they are stoned), three quarters of a pound of sugar, eight ounces of suet, one nutmeg, and a quarter of a teaspoonful of salt. Put the pudding into a well-floured cloth, tie it up very closely, and boil it for four hours. The correspondent to whom we are indebted for this receipt says, that the cost of the ingredients does not exceed half a crown, and that the pudding is of sufficient size for a party of sixteen persons. We can vouch for its excellence, but as it is rather apt to break when turned out of the cloth, a couple of eggs would perhaps improve it. It is excellent cold. Sweetmeats, brandy, and spices can be added at pleasure.

Mashed potatoes, 1 lb.; carrots, 8 oz.; flour, 1 lb.; suet, $\frac{1}{2}$ lb.; sugar, $\frac{3}{4}$ lb.; currants and raisins, 1 lb. each; nutmeg, 1; little salt: 4 hours.

Most Victorians, however, would have settled for a more conventional recipe such as Mrs Agnes B. Marshall's:

PLUM PUDDING.

Ingredients: one and three-quarter pounds of chopped beef suet, three-quarters of a pound of freshly made white bread crumbs, six ounces of flour, a quarter of a pound of Brown and Polson's cornflour, three-quarters of a pound of stoned raisins, a quarter of a pound of chopped almonds, three-quarters of a pound of currants, washed and dried, three-quarters of a pound of sultanas, one pound of chopped apples, half a pound of chopped mixed peel, one pound of moist sugar, the juice of two lemons, the peel of two lemons, cut fine and chopped, one nutmeg grated, half a pound of crème de riz, two wine glasses of Silver Rays (white) rum, half a pint of milk, six whole eggs, and two ounces of Cowan's baking powder.

Mix these ingredients well together in a basin, then tie them up tightly in a clean pudding-cloth that is dusted over with flour and brown sugar, put it into boiling water, and boil for about twelve hours. The pudding may also be boiled in a basin, in which case the basin should be buttered and then dusted over inside with Demerara sugar, and the ingredients put in and the cloth tied over. When the pudding is cooked, turn it out, dust it over with a little caster sugar, and serve brandy or Silver Rays (white) rum butter with it.

106 A toast to Christmas while the pudding is cut.

Mince pies were just as indispensable as the plum pudding to the well-ordered Victorian Christmas lunch or dinner. In the early part of Victoria's reign they appeared on the Royal Christmas Day menus in preference to plum pudding. Mrs Marshall, who ran a school of cookery in London's Mortimer Street, published the following recipe for mince pies in her cookery book:

MINCE PIES.

Ingredients for mincemeat:—One and a half pounds of lean underdone roast beef, two pounds of beef suet, one pound of stoned raisins, one pound of picked sultanas, one and a half pounds of apples, one and a half pounds of pears, one pound of mixed peel, three quarters of a pound of blanched and chopped Valencia almonds, the thin peel of two oranges and two lemons. All the before-mentioned ingredients are to be chopped and then mixed with one pound of well washed and dried currants, a quarter of an ounce of mixed powdered spice, the juice from the lemons and oranges, one and a half pounds of Demerara sugar, half a pint of brandy, half a pint of sherry, half a pint of port, one wineglassful each of Marshall's maraschino syrup and noyeau syrup, and a quarter of a pint of Silver Rays (white) rum.

107 *Pièce de résistance!* Even in less affluent households no expense was spared over the Christmas dinner (*c.* 1860).

Make some puff paste, roll it out a quarter of an inch thick, and line some little plain or fancy pattypans with it; place a teaspoonful or dessertspoonful, or more, of mincemeat in each, according to its size, wet the edges of the paste and cover the mincemeat over with more paste; brush over the top with beaten-up whole raw egg, and put them in a quick oven for about five minutes, then take them out, dust them over with icing sugar to glaze them, and put them back to bake for fifteen to twenty minutes. Dish up in a pile on a dish-paper or napkin, and serve hot.

In the latter half of the nineteenth century the turkey began to make its appearance on the menus of middle-class families on Christmas Day with, of course, a full supporting cast of *relevés, entremets* etc. The turkey had arrived in the eastern counties of England in the sixteenth century by a rather circuitous route. Discovered by the Spanish invaders in South America it was brought by them to the Spanish Netherlands and made its way, along with Dutch bulbs, to these shores. But it was not until the late nineteenth century that it became really popular and within the financial grasp of the majority of Christmas revellers.

In America, on the other hand, turkey was plentiful and relatively cheap. Its size and its magnificent plumage made it the perfect festal bird, and turkey shoots were among the pre-Christmas activities long before the bird became popular in this country. But by the 1880s most Victorian families would have had a turkey on the Christmas Day menu, and Eliza Acton in her *Modern Cookery for Private Families* gives the following recipe for it:

ROAST TURKEY.

In very cold weather a turkey in its feathers will hang (in an airy larder) quite a fortnight with advantage; and however fine a quality of bird it may be, unless sufficiently long kept, it will prove not worth the dressing, though it should always be perfectly sweet when prepared for the table. Pluck, draw, and singe it with exceeding care; wash, and then dry it thoroughly with clean cloths, or merely wipe the outside well, without wetting it, and pour water plentifully through the inside. Fill the breast with forcemeat, or with the finest sausagemeat, highly seasoned with minced herbs, lemon rind, mace, and cayenne. Truss the bird firmly, lay it to a clear sound fire, baste it constantly and bountifully with butter, and serve it when done with good brown gravy, and well-made bread sauce. An entire chain of delicate fried sausages is still often placed in the dish round a turkey as garnish.

It is usual to fold and fasten a sheet of buttered writing paper over the breast to prevent its being too much coloured: this should be removed twenty minutes before the bird is done. A forcemeat of chestnuts may be very advantageously substituted for the commoner kinds in stuffing it, and the body may then be filled with chestnuts, previously stewed until tender in rich gravy, or simmered over a low fire in plenty of rasped bacon, with a high seasoning of mace, nutmeg, and cayenne, until they are so; or, instead of this, well-made chestnut sauce, or a dish of stewed chestnuts, may be sent to table with the turkey.

But the turkey would have been by no means the only course. For a well-to-do Victorian family, a Christmas lunch or dinner could well have comprised these additional items: vegetable soup, oyster patties, boiled leg of mutton and port jelly in addition to the traditional plum pudding and mince pies. Such a number of courses would not have been considered excessive except, perhaps, by the kitchen staff and the cook who had to struggle with the following recipes:

VEGETABLE SOUP.

Take two large carrots, two large onions, two peeled potatoes, two large turnips, two leeks, a sprig of thyme, and parsley, a handful of tarragon and chervil, two bay leaves, a good bunch of watercress and a dust of coralline pepper; fry well in two ounces of butter, add one tablespoonful of crême de riz and three pints of milk; let these cook very gently till tender, which will take about three-quarters of an hour, then tammy, and make hot in the bain marie and to each quart of the hot puree take half a pint of warm cream which has been mixed on to three raw yolks of eggs and one ounce of butter and strain this into the hot puree, and stir in the bain marie until the whole thickens; strain the soup into the soup tureen, and add a julienne garnish. This soup can also be prepared with stock instead of milk.

OYSTER PATTIES.

Roll your puff paste six times, cut with a round tin cutter about five inches in diameter, glaze with the white of an egg, then press a smaller round cutter in the centre, enough to cut the paste slightly, this will form the cover to your patty; Bake by a brisk fire, when done cut out the covers with a sharp penknife, be careful to leave a little paste to form the bottom of the patty. Have some oysters and chopped button mushrooms ready, warmed in bechamel sauce, fill the patties and serve very hot.

BOILED LEG OF MUTTON WITH CAPER SAUCE.

Take a well-hung leg of mutton, trim it as for roasting, cutting away the meat from the knuckle-bone, then put it into a clean cloth and tie it up, place it into a stewpan with enough boiling water to cover it, and salt to season, also some perfectly fresh, well-cleaned and prettily cut vegetables, such as celery, carrot, leeks, turnips, onions, herbs—thyme, bay leaf, parsley, peppercorns, and cloves; bring to the boil, then skim well and allow the meat to simmer on the side of the stove very gently for two and a half to three hours, according to the size of the joint, then when cooked take up, remove the cloth, and place the leg on a very hot dish, pour a little of the strained gravy round it and garnish with the vegetables, serve with caper sauce in a sauce boat. The liquor from the boiling can be used for mutton broth.

PORT JELLY.

To one pint of clarified syrup, add two ounces of clarified isinglass, the filtered juice of two lemons, and a gill and a half of port. Pour this into a jelly mould ready set in rough ice.

And after the port jelly, the plum pudding and mince pies, came nuts, fruit and port or, in some houses, hot toddy, wassail or mulled wine:

> At last the dinner was all done, the cloth was cleared, the hearth swept, and the fire made up. The compound in the jug being tasted and considered perfect, apples and oranges were put upon the table, and a shovelful of chestnuts on the fire. Then all the Cratchit family drew round the hearth, in what Bob Cratchit called a circle, meaning half a one; and at Bob Cratchit's elbow stood the family display of glass—two tumblers, and a custard-cup without a handle. These held the hot stuff from the jug, however, as well as golden goblets would have done; and Bob served it out with beaming looks, while the chestnuts on the fire sputtered and cracked noisily.

From the Cratchit's homely fireside to the Banqueting Hall at Windsor Castle would have been a vast gastronomic step. On Christmas Day 1840, Queen Victoria sat down to dinner with eighteen of her family and friends including her young husband of ten months, her mother, Lord Melbourne, the Duchess of Bedford and Baroness Lehzen. The meal started with turtle soup. This was followed by a choice of haddock or sole, then by a choice of beef or roast swan. The next course provided a choice of veal, chicken, turbot, partridge or curried rabbit and this was followed by either pheasant or capon. The diners were then regaled with mince pies before settling in to a savoury or pudding. For those of the royal party who were still hungry, the side-table boasted roast beef, roast mutton, roast turkey, a chine of pork, turkey pie (containing turkey, larks and pheasants), partridge, brawn, sausages and boar's head.

It is interesting that turkey only made a guest appearance at this meal.

20. Everyone's idea of a perfect Father Christmas—from Pears' Christmas Annual, 1896.

21. A prosperous London family returning home after mattins on Christmas morning, 1855.

22. An idealised Christmas scene in the country.

23. Snowballing by the full moon, 1860.

24. A Victorian view of holly gathering in the late eighteenth century.

25. Mistletoe Galop—a Christmas music front.

26. The Snowman.

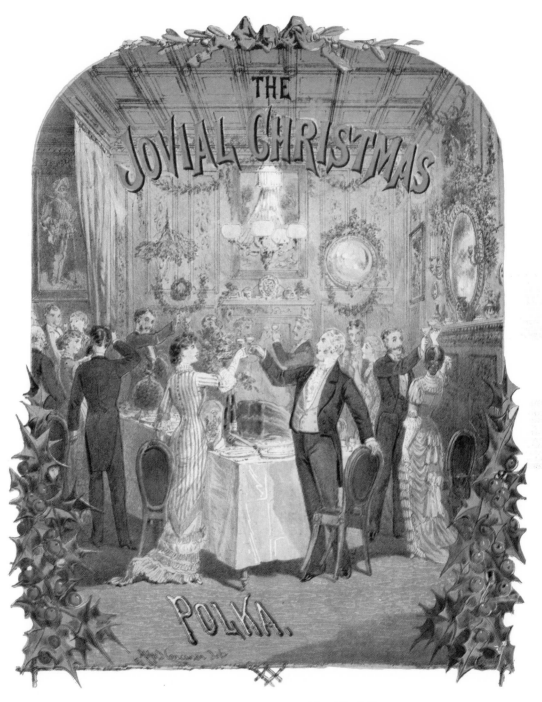

27. The Jovial Christmas as portrayed by Alfred Concanen.

28. Entertainment for a country squire.

29. Drawing lots for charades at a children's party on Twelfth Night.

108 Bringing in the boar's head at Queen's College, Oxford, a traditional Christmas ceremony still conducted today (*c.* 1850).

Friday 25th of Decr 1840 — Her Majesty's Dinner

Potages
À la Tortue
De Quenelles au Consommé

Poissons
Les Aigrefins, S. aux Câpres
Les Soles Frites, S. aux Crevettes

Relevés
La Pièce de Bœuf aux legumes
Le Cygne Rôti à l'Anglaise

Entrées
Les Tendons de Veau glacés
Les Filets de Poulets à la Maréchale
Le Ravi de Laperau à l'Indienne
La Pièce de Volaille aux Câpres
Les Filets de Turbot à la Richelieu
Les Escalopes de Perdreaux

Rôts
Les Faisans   Le Chapon

Relevés
Mince Pies
Le Pudding en Surprise

Entremets
Le Buisson de Truffes
Les Canapés d'Anchois
Les Croûtes aux Champignons
Les Épinards à la Crème
Les Casolettes Garnies
La Gelée de Pieds de Veau
Le Bavarois de Framboises
Les Merangues à la Chantilly
Les Choux aux Amandes

Side Table
B. Beef   Perdrix au jus
B. Mutton   Escalope de Bœuf
B. Turkey
Chine of Pork
Oxford Brawn
Boar's Head
Turkey Pie
Sausages

The Queen & Prince Albert
Duchess of Kent
Ld. Melbourne
Ld. & Ly. Kinnaird
Ld. Lilford
Duchess of Bedford
Sy. F. Howard
Miss Paget
Miss Cocks
Mr. & Mrs. Anson
Baroness Lehzen
Mr. Seymour
Mr. Murray
Col. Wemyss
Sir E. Bowater
Mr. Rich

109 Menus for Christmas Dinner at Windsor Castle in 1840 and 1851.

Thursday 25th December 1851

Her Majesty's Dinner.

26 — The Queen and Prince Albert.
Duchess of Kent.
Potages
Aux Quenelles à l'Allemande. — Baroness Spaeth.
Aux Escalopes de Ris de Veau. — Lady C. M. Dawson.
Poissons
Le Turbot bouilli. — Sir G. and Lady Couper.
Les Eperlans frits. — Col. and Mr. Bouverie.
— Col. and Mr. Phipps.
Relevés
Le Dindon farci rôti. — Lady and Miss Warrington.
La Carpe à la Chambord. — Lady Ely.
Entrées
— Miss Stanley.
La Grouse à la Financière. — Miss Wynn.
Les Poulets à la Périgueux. — Marquis of Ormonde.
Le Pâté de Porc aux fines herbes. — Gen. Wemyss.
La Chartreuse de Salmi de Sarcelles. — Col. Hood.
Le Hure de Chevreuil piquée. — Col. Grey.
Les Escalopes de Bœuf à la Chicorée — Mr. Wellesley.
La Suprème de Volaille aux Champignons — Dr. Becker.
Les Croquettes de Volaille. — Mr. Meyrick.
— Mr. Gibson.
Rôts
Les Chapons.   Les Wigeons.
Relevés
Le Soufflé à la Vanille.   Mince Pies.
Entremets
Les Bordures à la Moëlle.
Le Celeri frit.
La Dame d'Esturgeon.   The Royal Family.
L'Aspic de Galantine.
La Gelée de Fruit.
La Gelée de Champagne.
Le Blanc mangé.
La Chartreuse de Poires.
Les Nougats à la Crème.
Les Fanchonettes à l'Orange.
Les Mauches aux Cerises.
Les Choux pralinés
Side Table.
Sirloin of Beef   Boar's Head.
Chine of Mutton.   Brawn.
Baron of Beef. Chine & Mutton.
Boiled Turkey.
Game Pie.

In fact, roast turkey does not appear consistently on Royal Christmas Day Menus until 1851 when it replaced roast swan. The other mediaeval dish, boar's head, however, remained part of the traditional Christmas Day menu for very much longer. It is still brought in to Queen's College, Oxford, each year to the accompaniment of the famous 'Boar's Head Carol'—*Caput apri defero*. In 1898, when the Queen broke her usual habit and spent Christmas at Windsor, the boar for the royal table was shot in Windsor Great Park to the intense excitement of the citizens of Windsor, who were doubtless glad that they did not have to cook it:

BOAR'S HEAD.

Boil some laurel leaves, mixed herbs, heads of cloves, and whole black peppers, in very strong salt and water, pass through a tammy, and leave until cold. Singe and scrape the boar's head, be careful not to cut the skin, clean out the nostrils and ears with a hot iron, wash and bone the head, spread it out on a table, cut off all the flesh, and divide it into narrow fillets. Put the empty head to soak in the brine. Soak the fillets and a few slices of the boar's flesh in white wine, seasoned with onions, carrots, herbs, salt, pepper, and mixed spice; leave both head and fillets to soak for twenty-four hours, turn them occasionally, and when required for use, drain, dry, and spread them out on a table, with the inside of the head turned upwards. Have some fillets of rabbit, breasts of chicken and partridge, two sliced pickled tongues, and sliced truffles ready prepared; pound the carcases of the rabbits and birds in a mortar, with a few slices of veal and bacon; spread a layer of this forcemeat on the head, and fill it up with the fillets of boar, rabbit, chicken, partridge, tongue, and truffles; if there are any interstices stop them up with forcemeat, sew up the head to its original shape, tie it up tightly in a cloth, and place in a braising-pan with mirepoix made with Madeira; when cooked, drain it, tie a broad tape round the head, over the snout, leave for twenty-four hours, after which cut off the tape, cover the head with lard, and sprinkle with grated breadcrust.

From the boar's head to the humble goose was indeed a big step, but whatever the menu, the Christmas dinner was one meal the Victorians of all classes remembered all through the year until it was time once again to stir the pudding and roll out the pastry for the mince pies.

After Dinner.

Will you, won't you, will you, won't you,
Will you join the dance?

The Mock Turtle's Song, LEWIS CARROLL

WITH Christmas dinner over and the precious glasses carefully re-moved, the good Victorian father would have produced crackers. Originally unsophisticated indoor fireworks, by the later part of the nineteenth century they became, in the words of a contemporary writer, 'receptacles for bon-bons, rhymed mottoes, little paper caps and aprons and similar toys'. One popular type was the silhouette cracker—decorated with the silhouettes of well-known characters in the contemporary political, military or social world. When pulled they shed a shower of musical toys, cameos and bric-à-brac across the table, ending up, perhaps, where some-one was trying to light an indoor firework, set up the magic lantern or wind up the musical box.

The Victorian family was never at a loss for things to do after dinner. There were songs to sing, recitations to endure and games to play. At Christmas, the children might well have been seen and heard after the meal, and almost certainly the evening's entertainment would have started with some games for them. There would, of course, have been prizes for the winners and forfeits for the losers—yet one more toy to add to the treasured collection or the horror of having to recite the whole of 'The Village Blacksmith' while standing upon one leg!

One of the most popular of all Victorian Christmas games was 'Snap-dragon'. A shallow bowl filled with spirit and currants was put on the floor and the spirit was ignited. The players then tried to snatch the cur-rants out of the flames and put them into their mouths. The trick was to move quickly and to close the mouth over the burning currant and extinguish the flame. Victorian writers like 'Uncle Tom' of the *Illustrated London News* described the game with relish:

> The large pewter dish filled with spirit is placed on the floor and attracts the attention of all the party. The light is applied—the flame burns beautifully azure, tipped with amber and scarlet, and whisks and frisks in a manner delightful to contemplate... Throw in the plums (currants). The spirit burns, the dish is a lake of fire; and he who can gather the prize from the jaws of peril is welcome to it.
>
> 'Fortune favours the bold!' 'Faint heart never won a plum!'

An anonymous verse runs,

Here he comes with flaming bowl,
Don't he mean to take his toll,
   Snip! Snap! Dragon!
Take care you don't take too much,
Be not greedy in your clutch,
   Snip! Snap! Dragon!

With his blue and lapping tongue
Many of you will be stung,
   Snip! Snap! Dragon!
For he snaps at all that comes
Snatching at his feast of plums,
   Snip! Snap! Dragon!

But old Christmas makes him come,
Though he looks so fee! fa! fum!
   Snip! Snap! Dragon!
Don't 'ee fear him, be but bold—
Out he goes, his flames are cold,
   Snip! Snap! Dragon!

Variations on the old game of 'Blindman's Buff' were particularly enjoyed by the Victorians. 'Queen of Sheba' was an especially popular version in which the prettiest girl in the party was seated on a chair while the blindfolded player made his erratic way over to her to claim a kiss. However, at the last moment she was replaced by an aged relative, to the intense amusement of all. With all its variations, however, it was the original version of the game that enjoyed the greatest popularity:

> The very youngest of our brothers and sisters can join in this old English game: and it is selfish to select only such sports as they cannot become sharers of. Its ancient name is 'hoodman-blind'; and when hoods were worn by both

men and women—centuries before hats and caps were so common as they are now—the hood was reversed, placed hind-before, and was, no doubt, a much surer way of blinding the player than that now adopted—for we have seen Charley try to catch his pretty cousin Caroline, by chasing her behind chairs and into all sorts of corners, to our strong conviction that he was not half so well blinded as he ought to have been. Some said he could see through the black silk handkerchief; others that it ought to have been tied clean over his nose, for that when he looked down he could see her feet, wherever she moved; and Charley had often been heard to say that she had the prettiest foot and ankle he had ever seen. But there he goes, head over heels across a chair, tearing off Caroline's gown skirt in his fall, as he clutches it in the hope of saving himself. Now, that is what I call retributive justice; for she threw down the chair for him to stumble over, and, if he has grazed his knees, she suffers under a torn dress, and must retire until one of the maids darn up the rent. But now the mirth and glee grow 'fast and furious', for hoodman blind has imprisoned three or four of the youngest boys in a corner, and can place his hand on whichever he likes. Into what a small compass they have forced themselves! But the one behind has the wall at his back, and, taking advantage of so good a purchase, he sends his three laughing companions sprawling on the floor, and is himself caught through their having fallen, as his shoulder is the first that is grasped by Blindman-buff—so that he must now submit to be hooded.

For 'Hunt the Slipper' the players crouched in a circle surrounding one person. The slipper was passed around the circle out of sight of the player in the middle who had to guess at any moment who was in possession of it. This game, too, drew boundless enthusiasm from 'Uncle Tom':

> It is not a little amusing to note the struggle with pride that sometimes assumes a place upon the countenances of middle-aged and old people when they are pressed into the service of 'Hunt the Slipper', and how at last the solemn man of business, and the staid matron, yield to the solicitations and the example of the lighter-hearted folk around them and, with comic gravity, sit down on the floor and play their part in the game. A grave sergeant-at-law, or the elderly author of an incomparable and incomprehensible treatise upon metaphysics, or a spectacled physician of sixty sitting on his hams on a carpet, and passing the slipper under them with all the dexterity, if not with all the glee, of a school boy, is a sight to be enjoyed.

Perhaps the most popular of all games was Charades. Within the respectable confines of their own homes, respectable families could emulate those

110 Snapdragon was a favourite Christmas game. It involved picking currants out of a bowl of burning spirit and popping them into the mouth, thereby extinguishing the flame.

111 Blindman's buff – still a very popular children's game (1849).

112 Forfeits – the penalty for the loser (1849).

113 Acting a Christmas charade (1859).

114 The Christmas conjuror held children and adults spellbound with his amazing tricks and flourishes (1877).

115 The magic lantern show (1858).

138

116 Sometimes Victorian families performed elaborate ama-
teur theatricals at Christmas time. Here is 'Miss Hardcastle
in *She stoops to conquer* (1872).

Overleaf: The Victorians loved to gather round the piano on Christmas evening and sing familiar and topical songs. Here are two examples – the famous
'Mistletoe Bough' (**117**), and 'An English Christmas Home' (**118**).

No. 9.   # THE MISTLETOE BOUGH.

Published, with Words and Pianoforte Accomps., full Music size, in No. 3566 of the MUSICAL BOUQUET. Price 3d.

Composed by SIR H. R. BISHOP.

1. The mis-tle-toe hung in the cas - tle hall, The hol-ly branch shone on the old oak wall; And the
2. "I'm wea-ry of dan - cing now," she cried, "Here tar-ry a mo-ment, I'll hide, I'll hide! And

baron's re - tain-ers were blithe and gay, And keeping their Christmas ho - li-day. The baron beheld, with a fa - ther's pride, His
Lo-vel, be sure thou'rt the first to trace The clue to my se - cret lurk - ing place." A - way she ran and her friends be-gan Each

beau-ti-ful child, young Lo - vel's bride; While she with her bright eyes seem'd to be The star of the good - ly com-pa-ny.
tow-er to search, and each nook to scan; And young Lovel cried, "Oh! where dost thou hide? I'm lonesome without thee, my own dear bride."

Oh! the mistletoe bough! Oh! the mistletoe bough!

117

MADAME SAINTON-DOLBY'S POPULAR SONGS AND BALLADS.

Repeat from 𝄊 for 2nd verse. 2nd time.

They sought her that night! and they sought her next day! And they sought her in vain when a

week pass'd a - way! In the high-est, the low-est, the lone - li - est spot, Young Lov-el sought wildly, but found her not; And

Rather slow.

years flew by, and their grief at last Was told as a sor-row-ful tale long past; And when Lov-el appear'd, the children cried, "See! the

old man weeps for his fai - ry bride." Oh! the mis-tle-toe bough! Oh! the mis-tle-toe bough!

pp colla voce.

At length an oak chest, that had long laid hid, Was found in the cas-tle; they rais'd the lid, And a ske-le-ton form lay moul-d'ring there, In the bri-dal wreath of the la-dy fair! Oh! sad was her fate! in spor-tive jest She hid from her lord in the old oak-chest; It clos'd with a spring! and her bri-dal bloom Lay wi-ther-ing there in a liv-ing tomb. Oh! the mis-tle-toe bough! Oh! the mis-tle-toe bough!

118

who followed the least respectable of all professions—actors. The Victorians had many acting games, from the simple charade in which the syllables of words were acted out to be guessed to the most complicated staged productions. These charades varied between highly professional entertainment and mere dressing up. However enjoyable they may have been, the conscientious Victorian father would always have kept a cautious eye on the proceedings, aware of the possibility of the kind of accident which the Rev. W. F. Dawson reported in his book *Christmas, its origins and associations*:

FATALLY BURNT IN CHRISTMAS COSTUMES.

The Christmastide of 1885–6 was marred by two fatal accidents which again illustrate the danger of dressing for entertainments in highly-inflammable materials. In the first case a London lady, on Boxing Night, was entertaining some friends, and appeared herself in the costume of *Winter*. She was dressed in a white robe of thin fabric, and stood under a canopy from which fell pieces of cotton wool to represent snowflakes, and in their descent one of them caught light at the candelabra, and fell at deceased's feet. In trying to put it out with her foot her dress caught fire, and she was immediately enveloped in flames. So inflammable was the material that, although prompt assistance was rendered, she was so severely burnt as to become unconscious. A medical man was sent for, and everything possible was done for her; but she sank gradually, and died from exhaustion. The second of these tragical incidents plunged a Paris family in deep sorrow. The parents, who lived in a beautiful detached house in the Rue de la Bienfaisance, had arranged that their children and some youthful cousins were to play before a party of friends on New Year's Night on the stage of a little theatre which had just been added to their house. The play was to represent the decrepit old year going out and the new one coming in. The eldest daughter, a charming girl of fourteen, was to be the good genius of 1886, and to be dressed in a loose transparent robe. On the appointed evening, after the company had assembled, she donned her stage costume and ran into her mother's bedroom to see how it became her. While looking at herself in a mirror on the toilette table her loose sleeve came in contact with the flame of a candle and blazed up. She screamed for help and tried to roll herself in the bed clothes; but the bed, being covered with a lace coverlet and curtained with muslin was also set on fire, and soon the whole room was ablaze. By the time help arrived the girl's clothes were all burning into the flesh; but such was her vitality that, in spite of the dreadful state in which every inch of her body was, she survived the accident many hours.

Similar disasters occurred at Christmas festivities in 1889, at Detroit, and in 1891, at Wortley, Leeds. In the former several little children were fatally burnt, and in the latter fifteen children were set on fire, eleven of them fatally.

After the games and charades, it was time for the individual members of a family party to entertain the company. The main ingredient of Victorian home entertainment was undoubtedly the recitation or song. Everyone could play, sing or recite, and even if they couldn't do it very well they would all have made an attempt. But on Christmas night, if on no other, there was just the possibility that someone who couldn't play, sing or recite very well might be persuaded to perform some conjuring tricks. Many Victorian magazines contained instructions on how to perform some simple passes, and with a little practice a raffish uncle possessed of a mediocre baritone voice could acquit himself far better by 'teaching an egg to dance' or by displaying 'the affectionate card' or 'the penetrative shilling':

THE MAGIC OF TERPSICHORE; OR, HOW TO TEACH AN EGG TO DANCE.

Three eggs are brought out, and two of them are put on the table and the third in a hat; a little cane is borrowed from one of the company, and it is shown about, to convince the spectators that there has been no preparation. It is then placed across the hat, the hat falls to the ground, and the egg sticks to it as though it were glued. Then ask some one to play on the pianoforte, and the egg, as though sensible of the harmony, twists about the cane from one end to the other, and continues its gyrations till the music stops. The egg is fastened to a thread by a pin, which is put in lengthways; and the hole which has been made to introduce the pin is stopped with white wax. The other end of the thread is fastened to the breast of the person who performs the trick, with a pin bent like a hook: the thread passing under the cane near to the egg serves for it to rest upon. When the music begins the performer pushes the cane from right to left, and from left to right. It then appears as if the egg ran along the cane, which it does not: being fastened to the thread, its centre of gravity remains always at the same distance from the hook that holds it; it is the cane which, sliding along, presents its different points to the surface of the egg. To produce the illusion, and persuade the company that it is the egg that moves, the performer should turn a little on his heel. By this means the egg receives a deceptive motion.

THE AFFECTIONATE CARD.

This trick, if properly managed, will appear marvellous. Having forced a card upon one of the company, after shuffling it up with one of the pack, you will know the card by feeling. You then take a small piece of wax and place it under the thumbnail of your right hand, and by this wax you fasten one end of a hair to your thumb, and the other to the chosen card. By these means, when you spread your cards on the table, by drawing about your right hand, the chosen card will follow you all round the table, as though attracted by some magic sympathy.

THE PENETRATIVE SHILLING.

To perform this trick you must have a handkerchief with a counter the same size as the shilling, sewed up in one corner of it; take your handkerchief out of your pocket, and ask some person in company to lend you a shilling, which you must seem carefully to wrap up in the handkerchief, but at the same time keep the shilling in the palm of your hand, and in its stead wrap the corner in which the counter is sewed into the middle of the handkerchief, and bid the person who lent you the shilling feel that his money is there. Lay the handkerchief under a hat upon the table, take a glass or teacup in the hand that holds the shilling, place it under the shilling, under which knock three times, saying, 'Presto! come quickly!' Then let the shilling drop from your hand into the glass. Take the handkerchief by the corner that holds the counter and shake it, and the shilling not being there it will appear to have passed through the table into the glass or teacup.

After the display of conjuring, one member of the family would invariably move to the pianoforte and another would offer to sing. There were many songs with a Christmas flavour, but undoubtedly one of the Victorians' favourites was Sir Henry Bishop's 'The Mistletoe Bough'. After that the songs would follow thick and fast, the whole family joining in. There were songs from the Christmas numbers of periodicals to be tried out and songs written especially for children to sing. Finally when the singers and reciters were exhausted, and if the pianist could be prevailed upon, there might be dancing. In the words of 'Uncle Tom':

Hark! the sound of music: the dance begins; and Polka—the universal polka—summons all hands and feet to another celebration; and to a sport in comparison to which all others are of small account.

Interspersed with the songs, there were the recitations. Taking up a hefty tome entitled *The Elocutionist* or perhaps *The Home Reciter* the performer would select a poem or ballad either dramatic or didactic and begin to declaim in stentorian tones matching his bodily attitudes to the tone of the verse. The poetry of W. E. Henley with its high moral tone was an admirable vehicle for the impressive reader. 'England My England' was a particularly popular piece.

ENGLAND, MY ENGLAND.

What have I done for you,
　England, my England?
What is there I would not do,
　England, my own?
With your glorious eyes austere,
As the Lord were walking near,
Whispering terrible things and dear
　As the Song on your bugles blown,
　　England—
　Round the world on your bugles blown.

Where shall the watchful Sun
　England, my England,
Match the masterwork you've done,
　England, my own?
When shall he rejoice again
Such a breed of mighty men
As come forward, one to ten,
　To the Song on your bugles blown,
　　England—
　Down the years on your bugles blown?

Ever the faith endures,
　England, my England:—
'Take, and break us: we are yours,
　England, my own!
Life is good, and joy runs high

Between English earth and sky
Death is death; but we shall die
　To the Song on your bugles blown,
　　England—
　To the stars on your bugles blown!'

They call you proud and hard,
　England, my England:
You with worlds to watch and ward,
　England, my own!
You whose mailed hand keeps the keys
Of such teeming destinies
You could know nor dread nor ease
　Were the Song on your bugles blown,
　　England,
　Round the Pit on your bugles blown!

Mother of Ships whose might,
　England, my England,
Is the fierce old Sea's delight,
　England, my own,
Chosen daughter of the Lord,
Spouse-in-Chief of the ancient sword,
There's the menace of the Word
　In the Song on your bugles blown!
　　England—
　Out of heaven on your bugles blown!

But for sheer drama and pathos it was hard to better Longfellow. The accomplished reciter could command total attention with a blood-curdling rendering of 'The Wreck of the Hesperus'.

THE WRECK OF THE HESPERUS.

It was the schooner Hesperus,
    That sailed the wintry sea;
And the skipper had taken his little daughter,
    To bear him company.

Blue were her eyes as the fairy flax,
    Her cheeks like the dawn of day,
And her bosom white as the hawthorn-buds,
    That ope in the month of May.

The skipper he stood beside the helm,
    His pipe was in his mouth,
And he watched how the veering flaw did blow,
    The smoke now west, now south.

Then up and spake an old sailor,
    Had sailed the Spanish Main,
'I pray thee, put into yonder port,
    For I fear a hurricane.

'Last night, the moon had a golden ring,
    And tonight no moon we see!'
The skipper, he blew a whiff from his pipe,
    And a scornful laugh laughed he.

Colder and louder blew the wind,
    A gale from the north-east;
The snow fell hissing in the brine,
    And the billows frothed like yeast.

Down came the storm, and smote amain
    The vessel in its strength;
She shuddered and paused, like a frighted steed,
    Then leaped her cable's length.

'Come hither! come hither! my little daughter,
    And do not tremble so;
For I can weather the roughest gale,
    That ever wind did blow.'

He wrapped her warm in his seaman's coat,
    Against the stinging blast;
He cut a rope from a broken spar,
    And bound her to the mast.

'O father! I hear the church-bells ring,
    O say, what may it be?'
''Tis a fog-bell on a rock-bound coast!'—
    And he steered for the open sea.

'O father! I hear the sound of guns,
    O say what may it be?'
'Some ship in distress, that cannot live
    In such an angry sea!'

O father! I see a gleaming light,
    O say what may it be?'
But the father answered never a word,
    A frozen corpse was he.

Lashed to the helm, all stiff and stark,
    With his face turned to the skies,
The lantern gleamed through the gleaming sno
    On his fixed and glassy eyes.

Then the maiden clasped her hands and prayec
    That savèd she might be;
And she thought of Christ who stilled the wave
    On the lake of Galilee.

And fast through the midnight dark and drear,
　Through the whistling sleet and snow,
Like a sheeted ghost, the vessel swept
　Towards the reef of Norman's Woe.

And ever the fitful gusts between
　A sound came from the land;
It was the sound of the trampling surf,
　On the rocks and the hard sea-sand.

The breakers were right beneath her bows,
　She drifted a dreary wreck,
And a whooping billow swept the crew
　Like icicles from her deck.

She struck where the white and fleecy waves
　Looked soft as carded wool,
But the cruel rocks they gored her side
　Like the horns of an angry bull.

Her rattling shrouds, all sheathed in ice,
　With the masts went by the board;
Like a vessel of glass, she stove and sank,
　Ho! ho! the breakers roared!

At day-break, on the bleak sea-beach,
　A fisherman stood aghast,
To see the form of a maiden fair,
　Lashed close to a drifting mast.

The salt was frozen on her breast,
　The salt tears in her eyes;
And he saw her hair, like the brown sea-weed,
　On the billows fall and rise.

Such was the wreck of the Hesperus,
　In the midnight and the snow!
Christ save us all from a death like this,
　On the reef of Norman's Woe!

Following the entertainment and the dancing, cordials or punch would have been served and Christmas Day would draw, all too soon, to a close. The visitors made their way home and the family retired to bed:

Soon after ten o'clock the home-returning travellers begin to appear in the streets. Once more the wayfarers are almost without exception parcel-laden.

They are bearing back the gifts that have been presented to them in return for their own. Through the front door you occasionally catch a glimpse of the good-bye. There is considerable embracing among the ladies. The men shake hands with a hearty grip that has the sentiment of the season in it. The old four-wheel cabman sits nodding on his box. But even he revives under the influence of the proferred glass of grog, and wheezes out "the compliments of the season" between two coughs.

Soon after eleven o'clock the cats have the roadway to themselves. They dart from area to area undisturbed. Even the dogs seem to be keeping Christmas indoors.

Midnight strikes. You hear it in the silence of Christmas night as you hear it at no other time. The great day has come to an end. If you are abroad you will be startled by your own solitude. You will understand how truly is Christmas the festival of the home. A man or a woman alone kindles a feeling of sympathy in your breast; you begin to think a tragedy of friendlessness around them.

You pass the cab-stand. It is empty. You pass the public-house. It is shut. The buses have ceased running. You quicken your steps, and hasten to your own home, which you have only quitted because you want to see what London looks like on Christmas night. As you pass the policeman you involuntarily say, 'Merry Christmas to you.' The policeman answers, 'Same to you, sir.' Perhaps you put your hand in your pocket. It is past midnight, and Boxing Day has dawned.

119 The after-dinner singer prepares his audience with a few words of introduction, *c.* 1890.

150

Christmas Abroad.

From Greenland's icy mountains,
From India's coral strand...
BISHOP HEBER

HOW many Victorian families sitting down to their Christmas lunch were one or two members short? Christmas was a time for remembering absent friends and relatives—some of them perhaps spending Christmas abroad, still trying, in soaring temperatures, to re-create the atmosphere of Christmas at home: Douglas Sladen describes 'A Summer Christmas' in Australia:

The Christmas dinner was at two,
And all that wealth or pains could do
Was done to make it a success;
And marks of female tastefulness,
And traces of a lady's care,
Were noticeable everywhere.
The port was old, the champagne dry,
And every kind of luxury
Which Melbourne could supply was there.
They had the staple Christmas fare,
Roast beef and turkey (this was wild),
Mince-pies, plum-pudding, rich and mild,
One for the ladies, one designed
For Mr. Forte's severer mind,
Were on the board, yet in a way
It did not seem like Christmas day
With no gigantic beech yule-logs
Blazing between the brass fire-dogs,
And with 100° in the shade
On the thermometer displayed.
Nor were there Christmas offerings
Of tasteful inexpensive things,
Like those which one in England sends

At Christmas to his kin and friends,
Though the Professor with him took
A present of a recent book
For Lil and Madge and Mrs. Forte,
And though a card of some new sort
Had been arranged by Lil to face
At breakfast everybody's place.
When dinner ended nearly all
Stole off to lounges in the hall.
All save the two old folks and Lil,
Who made their hearts expand and thrill
By playing snatches, slow and clear,
Of carols they'd been used to hear
Some half a century ago
At High Wick Manor, when the two
Were bashful maidens: they talked on,
Of England and what they had done
On bygone Christmas nights at home,
Of friends beyond the Northern foam,
And friends beyond that other sea,
Yet further—whither ceaselessly
Travellers follow the old track,
But whence no messenger comes back.

The Victorians were fascinated by tales of Christmases spent abroad. December issues of the periodicals were full of stories of 'Christmas in Tibet', 'A seasonal visit to Christmas Island' or 'Christmas in a besieged Paris'. One correspondent in New Zealand, W. M. Stanton, started an article in 1887 with an idealized memory of Christmas in England which must have appealed strongly to his readers:

CHRISTMAS IN NEW ZEALAND.

And now, as to Christmas, I wish I could express all I feel on this peculiarly English season of 'peace and goodwill'. I remember the picturesque snow (seen here only on the distant blue mountain tops), the icy stalactites pendant from the leafless branches, the twitter of the robin redbreast, the holly, and the mistletoe, decorated homes, redolent with the effects of the festive cooking, and the warm blazing firelight, the meeting of families and of friends, the waits, the grand old peals from the belfries; but, alas, here these childhood associations are dispelled, half broken, and we acclimatised denizens adapt our festivities to other modes—not that we forget the Christmas season, but enjoy it differently, as I will briefly tell you. First, our ladies decorate the churches for the Christmas services, not with the evergreens of old exclusively; they do indeed affect the holly, ivy, and (New Zealand) mistletoe, but they make up with umbrageous and rich ferns, lachipoden, lauristinas, Portugal laurels, and our own beautiful evergreen, Ngaio, and with all the midsummer flowers at command; then the clerk, the storeman, the merchant, and the mechanic indulge in 'trips', or day excursions, in small steamboats, to the neighbouring bays surrounding small townships, and villages on the coast. Others again, take the train for a day's outing and play quoits, rounders, lawn tennis, and the like; the sportsman, perhaps, preferring his gun and his dog; families, again, are picnic-mad, for your colonist can rival the Cockney any day for making his holiday in the country. It may be to 'the rocks' he goes to watch his youngsters paddling in the rolling tide, or to the toil of clambering up the 'dim mountain', which seems to suit their hardy lungs better than the shade of the 'fern glen', and a journey of eighteen miles to the Maori Pa is as nothing. The Union Company's fine coasting steamships run passengers at half fares at this season, and the result is an interchange of visits between the dwellers in Nelson, Wellington, Marlboro', and Wanjani, amongst whom there is much rivalry and more friendship. Then there is the Christmas regatta, the performance of the 'Messiah' by the musical societies, and the inevitable evening dances, and thus the New Zealand Christmas is spent.

120 Christmas morning in the colonies (1890).

121 *Top right:* Christmas in Hudson Bay – a toast from the trappers (*c.* 1876).

122 Christmas morning under the starlit skies of Australia and on the frozen slopes of the Canadian Rockies (*c.* 1870).

And in her book *Sunshine and Storm in the East, or Cruises to Cyprus and Constantinople*, Lady Brassey gives a tantalizing glimpse of an English Christmas Day re-created on board the *Sunbeam* somewhere between Malta and Marseilles:

> December 25th 1879—
> We had service early and then spent a long busy morning in arranging all the presents for the children, servants, and crew, and in decorating the cabin. We could not manage any holly, but we had carefully preserved one bough of mistletoe from Artaki Bay, and had brought on board at Malta baskets full of flowers, so that all the pictures, lamps, and even walls, were wreathed with festoons of bougainvillæa, ivy, and other creeping plants; while in every available corner were placed, vases, bowls, and soup-plates, containing flowers. If not exactly 'gay with hollyberries', so dear to English hearts from their association with yule-tide at home, the general appearance of the cabins was highly satisfactory. In the meantime they had been busy in the kitchen and pantry departments, preparing all sorts of good things for dinner, and pretty things for dessert, in order that the crew and servants might enjoy a more sumptuous repast than usual. A Christmas tree, a snow man, or an ice cave, for the distribution of presents, was not within the limit of our resources; but we decorated our tables and sideboards with bright shawls and scarves, and wreathed and divided the surface of each with garlands of flowers, placing in every division a pretty Christmas card, bearing the name of the recipient of the present, which was hidden away among the flowers beneath.... For the men there was plenty of tobacco, besides books and useful things; for the children toys; and for ourselves, slippers and little remembrances of various kinds, some sent from home to meet us, others recent purchases. The distribution over, one or two speeches were made, and mutual congratulations and good wishes were exchanged. Then the crew and servants retired to enjoy the, to them, all-important event of the day—dinner and dessert. After our own late dinner, we thought of those near and dear to us at home, and drank to the health of 'absent friends'.

In 1870, just before the outbreak of the Franco-Prussian War, the Prussians sent out two ships, the *Germania* and the *Hansa*, to attempt to reach the North Pole. When one of the officers on the *Germania* wrote an article about Christmas in the Arctic regions, it was seized upon eagerly and translated for English readers:

> To the men who had already lived many weary months among the icebergs, Christmas signifies, in addition to its other associations, that the half of their

long night—with its fearful storms, its enforced cessation of all energy, its discomfort and sadness—has passed, and that the sun will soon again shed its life and warmth-giving beams on the long-deserted North. From this time the grim twilight, during which noon has been hardly distinguishable from the other hours, grows daily lighter, until at length all hearts are gladdened, and a cheerful activity is once again called forth by the first glimpse of the sun. Christmas, the midnight of the Arctic explorer, thus marks a period in his life which he has good cause to consider a joyful one.

For days before the festival, an unusual activity was observable all over the ship; and as soon as the severe storm which raged from December 16th to 21st had abated, parties were organised, under our botanist, Dr. Pansch, to certain points of Sabine Island, near to which we were anchored, where, in a strangely sheltered nook, several varieties of a native Greenland evergreen plant, *Andromeda tetragona*, were to be found. A great quantity of this plant was conveyed on board, to be converted into a Christmas-tree. Under the orders of Dr. Pansch, the Andromeda was wound round small pieces of wood, several of which were attached, like fir-twigs, to a large bough; and when these boughs were fastened to a pole, they formed a very respectable fir-tree.

After dinner on Christmas Day, the cabin was cleared for the completion of the preparations; and on our recall at six o'clock, we found that all had assumed an unwontedly festive appearance. The walls were decorated with the signal-flags and our national eagle; and the large cabin table, somewhat enlarged to make room to seat seventeen men, was covered with a clean white cloth, which had been reserved for the occasion. On the table stood the 'fir' tree, shining in the splendour of many little wax-lights, and ornaments with all sorts of little treasures, some of which, such as the gilded walnuts, had already seen a Christmas in Germany; below the tree was a small present for each of us, provided long beforehand, in readiness for the day, by loving friends and relatives at home. There was a packet too for each of the crew, containing some little joking gift, prepared by the mirth-loving Dr. Pansch, and a useful present also; while the officers were each and all remembered.

When the lights burned down, and the resinous Andromeda was beginning to take fire, the tree was put aside, and a feast began, at which full justice was done to the costly Sicilian wine with which a friend had generously supplied us before we left home. We had a dish of roast seal! Some cakes were made by the cook, and the steward produced his best stores. For the evening, the division between the fore and aft cabins was removed, and there was free intercourse between officers and men; many a toast was drunk to the memory of friends at home, and at midnight a polar ball was improvised by a dance on the ice. The boatswain, the best musician of the party, seated himself with his hand-organ between the antlers of a reindeer which lay near the ship, and the men danced two and two on their novel flooring of hard ice!

123 A dignified picnic beside the lake for Australian families on Christmas Day (*c.* 1871) ...

124 ... A much more informal picnic down 'at the diggings' (1855).

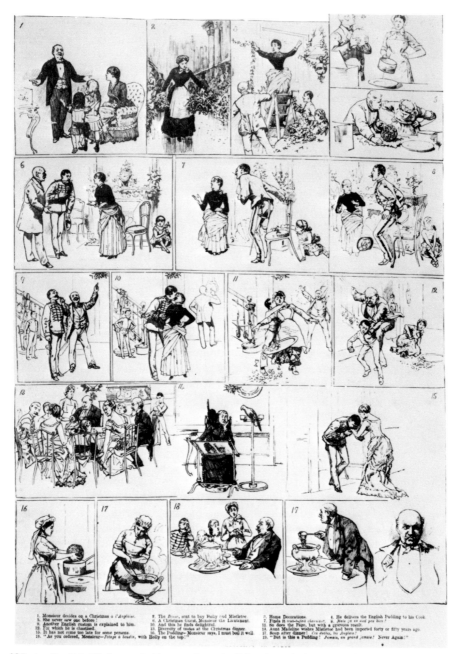

125 An English Christmas in France, from 1: 'Monsieur decides on a Christmas *à l'Anglaise*' to 19: 'But is this a pudding? *Jamais, au grand jamais!* Never again!' (1883).

And for those with a taste for adventure., the *English Illustrated Magazine* published in 1885 an article by Archibald Forbes entitled 'Christmastide in the Khyber Pass'.

Tytler determined to make his exit from the Zukkur-Kahl Valley by a previously unexplored pass, toward which the force moved for its night's bivouac. About the entrance to the glen there was a fine forest of ilex and holly, large, sturdy, spreading trees, whence dangled long sprays of mistletoe; the mistletoe bough was here indeed, and Christmas was close, but where the fair ones whom, under other circumstances, the amorous youth of our column would have so enthusiastically led under that spray which accords so sweet a license? The young ones prattled of those impossible joys; but the seniors, less frivolous, were concerned by the increasing narrowness of the gorge, and by the dropping fire that hung on our skirts as we entered it. However, there was but one casualty—a poor fellow of the 17th Regiment had his thigh smashed by a bullet—and we spent the night under the ilex trees without further molestation.... It was Christmas Eve when we sat chatting with young Beatson in his lonely post by the Chardai streamlet; but a few hours of morning riding would carry us to Jellalabad whither Sir Sam Browne's camp had been advanced, and we were easy on the score of being true to tryst. As in the cold grey dawn we resumed our journey, leaving the young officer who had been our host to concern himself with the watchfulness of his picquets and the vigilance of his patrols, there was a sound of unintentional mockery in the conventional wish of a 'Merry Christmas' to the gallant lad, and there was a wistfulness in his answering smile.... The road to the encampment, the white canvas of whose tents showed through the intervening hills, was traversed at a hand gallop; and presently Kinloch and myself found ourselves in the street of the headquarter camp, shaking hands with friends and comrades, and trying to reply to a medley of disjointed questions. The bugles were sounding for the Christmas Day Church Parade as we finished a hurried breakfast. Out there on the plain the British troops of the division were standing in hollow square, the officer grouped in the centre.... The headquarter street we found swept and garnished, the flagstaff bedecked with holly, and a regimental band playing 'Home, Sweet Home'. Dear old Sir Sam Browne did not believe in luxury when on campaign, but now for the first time I saw him at least comfortable.... The mess ante-room was the camp street outside the dining tent; and at the fashionable late hour of eight we 'went in' to dinner, to the strains of the *Roast Beef of Old England*. It was a right jovial feast, and the most cordial good-fellowship prevailed. He would have been a cynical epicurean who would have criticised the appointments; the banquet itself was above all cavil. Rummaging among some old papers the other day, I found the *menu*, which deserves to be quoted: 'Soup—Julienne. Fish—Whitebait (from the Cabul

River). Entrées—Cotelettes aux Champignons, Poulets à la Mayonaise. Joints—Ham and fowls, roast beef, roast saddle of mutton, boiled brisket of beef, boiled leg of mutton and caper sauce. Curry—chicken. Sweets—Lemon jelly, blancmange, apricot tart, plum-pudding. Grilled sardines, cheese fritters, cheese, dessert'. Truth compels the avowal that there was no table-linen, nor was the board resplendent with plate or gay with flowers. Table crockery was deficient, or to be more accurate, there was none. All the dishes were of metal, and the soup was eaten, or rather drunk, out of mugs and iron tea-cups. But it tasted none the worse on this account, and let it be recorded that there *were* champagne glasses, while between every two guests a portly magnum reared its golden head. Except 'The Queen', of course, there were but two toasts after the feast—one was 'Absent Friends', drunk in a wistful silence, and the other, the caterer's health, greeted with vociferous enthusiasm. A few fields off the wood had been collecting all day for the Christmas camp-fire of the 10th Hussars, and by ten o'clock the blaze of it was mounting high into the murky gloom. A right merry and social gathering it was round the bright glow of this Yule log in a far-off land. The flames danced on the wide circle of bearded faces, on the tangled fleeces of the postheens, on the gold braid of the forage caps, on the sombre hoods of beshliks. . . . The songs ranged from gay to grave; the former mood in the ascendency. But occasionally there was sung a ditty, the associations with which brought it about that there came something strangely like a tear into the voice of the singer, and that a yearning wistfulness fell upon the faces of the listeners. The bronzed troopers in the background shaded with their hands the fire-flash from their eyes; and as the familiar homely strain ceased that recalled home and love and trailed at the heart strings till the breast felt to heave and the tears to rise, there would be a little pause of eloquent silence which told how thoughts had gone astraying half across the globe to the loved ones in dear old England, and were loath to come back again to the rum and the camp fire in Jellalabad plain.

And so, while the Victorians at home in the mother country thought of their friends and relatives in other climes, those same friends and relatives thought of them. Christmas, above all times in the year, produced an orgy of nostalgia. While Englishmen in England raised their glasses to absent friends, Englishmen in the far-flung corners of the Empire raised theirs. The regimental band played 'Home, Sweet Home', Lady Brassey decorated the Christmas table aboard the *Sunbeam* and New Zealanders performed 'Messiah' as the temperature soared to 100° in the shade. And all dreamed of the Christmas to come when they would be reunited in the bliss of an English Christmas at home.

Christmas Charity.

◆

Go your way, eat of the fat and drink of the sweet,
and send portions to those for whom nothing is provided.

NEHEMIAH

◆

CHRISTMAS has always been a time for charity. Following the example of their Queen who annually distributed her Royal Bounty to well over 2000 people, the Victorians threw themselves into charitable works with enthusiasm, giving Christmas Boxes—presents of food and money—to all the deserving poor of the parish, usually on the day after Christmas. And there were in nineteenth-century England any number of deserving poor—amongst whom were the so-called 'parish officers', the lamplighter, the turncock, the parish beadle, the watchman, the dustman, the crossing-sweeper and many more. Workhouses and hostels for the poor were often visited by the well-to-do on Christmas Day as George R. Sims reports:

> From one to half-past there is a little stream of visitors to the workhouse and certain charitable institutions, where Christmas is being celebrated by a dinner to the inmates. Fashionable philanthropy which has contributed to the good cheer passes a pleasant half-hour on Christmas Day in assisting the poor, the lonely, and the afflicted to share in the common joy. Even in the great palaces of pain, where suffering is ever present and death rarely absent, the doctors, the nurses and the students do their best to bring a little of the world's happiness to the bedside of the patient. For the children there are toys and Christmas trees, for the grown-up folk such fare and amusement as they can appreciate.

But Victorian charity was not always unmingled with hypocrisy. In his poem, 'In the Workhouse—Christmas Day' Sims points out with a poignant pen that charity on Christmas Day often came too late:

126 Visiting the poor – the act of charity the Victorians frequently carried out the day after Christmas (*c.* 1870).

127 Coal was distributed to the poor and needy under the supervision of the Beadle as an act of Christmas charity (1849).

128 'A Utopian Christmas' – the dream of every beggar and street urchin. And, no doubt, what every member of the affluent middle classes, with a conscience, would have wanted to provide for them (1859).

129 A street fiddler, with his younger brother, gaze longingly at the good things displayed in the grocer's window (1876).

IN THE WORKHOUSE.

CHRISTMAS DAY

It is Christmas Day in the Workhouse,
    And the cold bare walls are bright
With garlands of green and holly,
    And the place is a pleasant sight:
For with clean-washed hands and faces,
    In a long and hungry line
The paupers sit at the tables,
    For this is the hour they dine.

And the guardians and their ladies,
    Although the wind is east,
Have come in their furs and wrappers,
    To watch their charges feast;
To smile and be condescending,
    Put pudding on pauper plates,
To be hosts at the workhouse banquet
    They've paid for—with the rates.

Oh, the paupers are meek and lowly
    With their 'Thank'ee kindly, mum's';
So long as they fill their stomachs,
    What matter it whence it comes?
But one of the old men mutters,
    And pushes his plate aside:
'Great God!' he cries; 'but it chokes me!
    For this is the day *she* died.'

The guardians gazed in horror,
    The master's face went white;
'Did a pauper refuse their pudding?'
    'Could their ears believe aright?'
Then the ladies clutched their husbands,
    Thinking the man would die,
Struck by a bolt, or something,
    By the outraged One on high.

But the pauper sat for a moment,
    Then rose 'mid a silence grim,
For the others had ceased to chatter,
    And trembled in every limb.
He looked at the guardians' ladies,
    Then, eyeing their lords, he said,
'I eat not the food of villains
    Whose hands are foul and red:

'Whose victims cry for vengeance
    From their dank, unhallowed graves.'
'He's drunk!' said the workhouse master.
    'Or else he's mad, and raves.'
'Not drunk, or mad,' cried the pauper,
    'But only a hunted beast,
Who, torn by the hounds and mangled,
    Declines the vulture's feast.

'I care not a curse for the guardians,
    And I won't be dragged away.
Just let me have the fit out,
    It's only on Christmas Day
That the black past comes to goad me,
    And prey on my burning brain;
I'll tell you the rest in a whisper,—
    I swear I won't shout again.

'Keep your hands off me, curse you!
    Hear me right out to the end.
You come here to see how paupers
    The season of Christmas spend.
You come here to watch us feeding,
    As they watch the captured beast.
Hear why a penniless pauper
    Spits on your paltry feast.

'Do you think I will take your bounty,
  And let you smile and think
You're doing a noble action
  With the parish's meat and drink?
Where is my wife, you traitors—
  The poor old wife you slew?
Yes, by the God above us,
  My Nance was killed by you!

Last winter my wife lay dying,
  Starved in a filthy den;
  had never been to the parish,—
I came to the parish then.
I swallowed my pride in coming,
  For, ere the ruin came,
I held up my head as a trader,
  And I bore a spotless name.

'I came to the parish, craving
  Bread for a starving wife,
Bread for the woman who'd loved me
  Through fifty years of life;
And what do you think they told me,
  Mocking my awful grief?
That "the House" was open to us,
  But they wouldn't give "out relief".

'I slunk to the filthy alley—
  'Twas a cold, raw Christmas eve—
And the bakers' shops were open,
  Tempting a man to thieve;
But I clenched my fists together,
  Holding my head awry,
So I came to her empty-handed,
  And mournfully told her why.

'Then I told her "the House" was open;
  She had heard of the ways of *that*,
For her bloodless cheeks went crimson,
  And up in her rags she sat,
Crying, "Bide the Christmas here, John,
  We've never had one apart;
I think I can bear the hunger,—
  The other would break my heart."

'All through that eve I watched her,
  Holding her hand in mine,
Praying the Lord, and weeping
  Till my lips were salt as brine.
I asked her once if she hungered,
  And as she answered "No,"
The moon shone in at the window
  Set in a wreath of snow.

'Then the room was bathed in glory,
  And I saw in my darling's eyes
The far-away look of wonder
  That comes when the spirit flies;
And her lips were parched and parted,
  And her reason came and went,
For she raved of our home in Devon,
  Where our happiest years were spent.

'And the accents, long forgotten,
  Came back to the tongue once more,
For she talked like the country lassie
  I woo'd by the Devon shore.
Then she rose to her feet and trembled,
  And fell on the rags and moaned,
And, "Give me a crust—I'm famished—
  For the love of God!" she groaned.

'I rushed from the room like a madman,
  And flew to the workhouse gate,
Crying, "Food for a dying woman!"
  And the answer came, "Too late."
They drove me away with curses;
  Then I fought with a dog in the street,
And tore from the mongrel's clutches
  A crust he was trying to eat.

'Back, through the filthy by-lanes!
  Back, through the trampled slush!
Up to the crazy garret,
  Wrapped in an awful hush.
My heart sank down at the threshold,
  And I paused with a sudden thrill,
For there in the silv'ry moonlight
  My Nance lay, cold and still.

'Up to the blackened ceiling
  The sunken eyes were cast—
I knew on those lips all bloodless
  My name had been the last;
She'd called for her absent husband—
  O God! had I but known!—
Had called in vain, and in anguish
  Had died in that den—*alone*.

'Yes, there, in a land of plenty,
  Lay a loving woman dead,
Cruelly starved and murdered
  For a loaf of the parish bread.
At yonder gate, last Christmas,
  I craved for a human life.
You, who would feast us paupers,
  What of my murdered wife!

'There, get ye gone to your dinners;
  Don't mind me in the least;
Think of the happy paupers
  Eating your Christmas feast;
And when you recount their blessings
  In your smug parochial way,
Say what you did for *me*, too,
  Only last Christmas Day.'

With some exceptions, charitable work was usually carried out on Boxing Day. Landlords and their families visited their tenants and brought gifts of food and drink, and middle-class families all over the country remembered their servants and the tradesmen who had served them faithfully over the year.

After Prince Albert's death in 1861, the Queen herself spent most of her Christmases at Osborne in the Isle of Wight where she could feel really secluded. As W. F. Dawson put it:

> The Queen desires to live, as far as the cares of State permit, the life of a private lady. Her Majesty loves the seclusion of this lordly estate, and here at Christmas time she enjoys the society of her children and grandchildren, who meet together as less exalted families do at this merry season to reciprocate the same homely delights as those which are experienced throughout the land.

Because of her wish for a quiet Christmas with her family, the Queen arranged to distribute her bounty to the children of the Osborne Estate on Christmas Eve. This custom is reported with enormous unction by an anonymous contemporary witness:

130 The Christmas Dole – the vicar ensures that the poor of his parish don't spend a joyless Christmas (1854).

131 The windmill and cup and ball that the old man has made for the children will surely bring happiness to both donor and receiver (1853).

This afternoon a pleasant little festivity has been celebrated at Osborne House, where her Majesty, with an ever-kindly interest in her servants and dependants, has for many years inaugurated Christmas in a similar way, the children of her tenantry and the old and infirm enjoying by the Royal bounty the first taste of Christmas fare. The Osborne estate now comprises 5,000 acres, and it includes the Prince Consort's model farm. The children of the labourers— who are housed in excellent cottages—attend the Whippingham National Schools, a pretty block of buildings, distant one mile from Osborne. About half the number of scholars live upon the Queen's estate, and, in accordance with annual custom, the mistresses of the schools, the Misses Thomas, accompanied by the staff of teachers, have conducted a little band of boys and girls— fifty-four in all—to the house, there to take tea and to receive the customary Christmas gifts. Until very recently the Queen herself presided at the distribution; but the Princess Beatrice has lately relieved her mother of the fatigue involved; for the ceremony is no mere formality, it is made the occasion of many a kindly word the remembrance of which far outlasts the gifts. All sorts of rumours are current on the estate for weeks before this Christmas Eve gathering as to the nature of the presents to be bestowed, for no one is supposed to know beforehand what they will be; but there was a pretty shrewd guess to-day that the boys would be given gloves, and the girls cloaks. In some cases the former had had scarves or cloth for suits, and the latter dresses or shawls. Whatever the Christmas presents may be, here they are, arranged upon tables in two long lines, in the servants' hall. To this holly-decorated apartment the expectant youngsters are brought, and their delighted gaze falls upon a huge Christmas-tree laden with beautiful toys. Everybody knows that the tree will be there, and moreover that its summit will be crowned with a splendid doll. Now, the ultimate ownership of this doll is a matter of much concern; it needs deliberation, as it is awarded to the best child, and the judges are the children themselves. The trophy is handed to the keeping of Miss Thomas, and on the next 1st of May the children select by their votes the most popular girl in the school to be elected May Queen. To her the gift goes, and no fairer way could be devised. The Princess Beatrice always makes a point of knowing to whom the prize has been awarded. Her Royal Highness is so constantly a visitor to the cottagers and to the school that she has many an inquiry to make of the little ones as they come forward to receive their gifts.

The girls are called up first by the mistress, and Mr. Andrew Blake, the steward, introduces each child to the Princess Beatrice, to whom Mr Blake hands the presents that her Royal Highness may bestow them upon the recipients with a word of good will, which makes the day memorable. Then the boys are summoned to participate in the distribution of good things, which, it should be explained, consist not only of seasonable and sensible clothing, but toys from the tree, presented by the Queen's grandchildren, who, with their parents, grace the ceremony with their presence and make the occasion one of family interest. The Ladies-in-Waiting also attend. Each boy and girl gets in addition a nicely-bound story-book and a large slice of plum pudding neatly packed in paper, and if any little one is sick at home its portion is carefully reserved. But the hospitality of the Queen is not limited to the children. On alternate years the old men and women resident on the estate are given, under the same pleasant auspices, presents of blankets or clothing. To-day it was the turn of the men, and they received tweed for suits. The aged people have their pudding as well. For the farm labourers and boys, who are not bidden to this entertainment, there is a distribution of tickets, each representing a goodly joint of beef for the Christmas dinner. The festivity this afternoon was brought to a close by the children singing the National Anthem in the courtyard.

And finally, if a Victorian child needed prompting in the direction of charity, Louisa M. Alcott's 'little women' gave a shining example. Not only did they go without Christmas presents, but they gladly gave away their breakfast as well when Mrs March described the plight of a poor family in the neighbourhood:

'Not far away from here lies a poor woman with a little new-born baby. Six children are huddled into one bed to keep from freezing, for they have no fire. There is nothing to eat over there; and the oldest boy came to tell me they were suffering hunger and cold. My girls, will you give them your breakfast as a Christmas present?'

They were all unusually hungry, having waited nearly an hour, and for a minute no one spoke; only a minute, for Jo exclaimed impetuously, 'I'm so glad you came before we began!'

'May I go and help carry the things to the poor little children?' asked Beth eagerly.

'I shall take the cream and the muffins,' added Amy, heroically giving up the articles she most liked.

Meg was already covering the buckwheats, and piling the bread into one big plate.

'I thought you'd do it,' said Mrs March, smiling as if satisfied. 'You shall all go and help me, and when we come back we will have bread and milk for breakfast, and make it up at dinner-time.'

A poor, bare, miserable room it was, with broken windows, no fire, ragged bed-clothes, a sick mother, wailing baby, and a group of pale hungry children huddled under one quilt, trying to keep warm. How the big eyes stared, and the blue lips smiled, as the girls went in!

'Ach, mein Gott! it is good angels come to us!' cried the poor woman, crying for joy.

'Funny angels in hoods and mittens,' said Jo, and set them laughing.

In a few minutes it really did seem as if kind spirits had been at work there. Hannah, who had carried wood, made a fire, and stopped up the broken panes with old hats and her own shawl. Mrs March gave the mother tea and gruel, and comforted her with promises of help, while she dressed the little baby as tenderly as if it had been her own. The girls, meantime, spread the table, set the children round the fire, and fed them like so many hungry birds; laughing, talking, and trying to understand the funny broken English.

'Das ist gute!' 'Der angel-kinder!' cried the poor things, as they ate, and warmed their purple hands at the comfortable blaze. The girls had never been called angel children before, and thought it very agreeable, especially Jo, who had been considered 'a Sancho' ever since she was born. That was a very happy breakfast, though they didn't get any of it; and when they went away, leaving comfort behind, I think there were not in all the city four merrier people than the hungry little girls who gave away their breakfasts and contented themselves with bread and milk.

Parties and Pantomimes.

---◆---

And now, good people, not to keep you long,
Pray, Mr Conductor, my favourite song.

---◆---

THE pantomime was one of the great Victorian institutions and a peculiarly British affair. Starting on Boxing Day in all the major theatres in the country, pantomimes attracted huge audiences of all generations. For the Victorian pantomime was pre-eminently family entertainment. It contained something for everyone and given a reasonable review in a national or local newspaper, and a fairly strong cast, any theatre manager could be certain of making a success of the season.

From its roots in the *commedia del arte* and less tangible areas the nine-teenth-century pantomime had grown into a vast complex mixture of fact and fiction, legend and history, tragedy and farce, in which the plot was always subordinate to almost everything else.

Lavishness was the order of the day. Any review that did not mention the scale and magnificence of the various transformation scenes, the vast number of players, the realism of the scenario and the breath-taking effects was worthless. The Victorians expected the grandiose in their pantomimes and valued it above all other considerations. The scenery had to astound, the masks and costumes had to astonish and the sound and lighting had to send a shiver down the spine.

Everything was calculated to titillate and excite the family audience. Even the title of the piece was adjustable to suit individual tastes. Thus Saddler's Wells in 1855 advertised their pantomime as 'The World and his Wife', 'Harlequin and Puss in Boots' or 'The Ogre of Rat's Castle'.

A complete pantomime diary for 1855 was given in the *Illustrated London News* and the Victorian family could browse at leisure through details of the plots, casts and spectacles of all the London shows. Eventually the choice was made, the tickets were bought and the date of the outing was awaited with excited anticipation:

THE PANTOMIMES.

Covent Garden.—The Great Wizard of the North has achieved a new triumph which will throw all his previous marvellous achievements into the shade. Finding, after the experience of a hundred and odd successive nights, the walls of the Lyceum Theatre too narrow to accommodate his numerous patrons, he resolved to remove to Covent Garden, and to add to the attractions of his feats of 'Magic and Mystery' a regular Christmas pantomime. The result has been a distinguished success, as well as a marvel of rapid organization; for, although the stage of this theatre had only been in his possession a clear week, the 'grand national historical and chivalric pantomime' of 'Ye Belle Alliance; or, Harlequin Good Humour and ye Fielde of ye Clothe of Golde,' was produced on Wednesday evening with a gorgeousness of scenic display, and a *luxe* of material and physical appliance which have seldom been surpassed, amid the boisterous plaudits of an audience packed to the ceiling. The subject of this pantomime is somewhat different from the ordinary run of Christmas entertainments. It aims at a higher object, and in place of a nursery fable adopts a grand political principle as its foundation—that involved in the friendly alliance now happily existing between the two great Western Powers. Opening with 'the Caverns of the Gnome *Britannicus* (Mr. J. Neville), in Subterraneanassia,' we are treated to a fine display of 'Old English' prejudice, which denounced everything foreign as abominable and unconstitutional—the aforesaid *Gnome's* uncontrollable wrath being excited at the news of Henry VIII's intended visit to Francis I of France, and he forthwith takes his departure in a dragon-car to thwart the project. Then comes *Good Humour*, in the person of Miss Harriet Gordon, who of course acts as the beneficent genius; and, amidst much vocalisation, displays a dioramic prophecy of the visit of Napoleon III to London, and that of Queen Victoria to Paris, where she inspects the tomb of the First Napoleon in the Invalides. We have next a very grand scene, an admirable mixture of pictorial effect, State pageantry, and comicality, 'The Deck of the *Great Harry*, four-decker, lying alongside the Quay at Dover', and the embarkation of Henry VIII (a part capitally filled by Mr. Harry Pearson), accompanied by his Queen, Cardinal Wolsey, and all his Court. An impromptu hornpipe, in which the 'Defender of the Faith' takes part, was a fine exhibition of artistic agility and genuine drollery. The scene of 'The Field of the Cloth of Gold', with the tournament after Holbein's celebrated picture at Hampton Court, was the next grand display, occupying the whole depth of the stage, the chivalric jousts being marked with a due infusion of mock gravity. The French Monarch, whose narrow angular physiognomy was in studied contrast to the expansive features of the merry Monarch, was played with considerable humour by Mr. W. Shalders, who only wants to 'speak louder' to be a favourite with the gods. 'A Pas de Rosière, introduced into this scene, by Miss Emma Horne (as *Blondette*, a young village lass, afterwards *Columbine*) and the corps de ballet, is an agreeable diversion, and is made to lead to the usual 'pantomimic changes', in the following manner;—the two monarchs are smitten with the charms of the young danseuse, and resolve to pay their addresses to her (each unknown to the other), sallying forth at night to serenade her at her farm, where all sorts of ignoble troubles and perils attend them. *Blondette*, of course, has a rustic lover, *Coquelicot*, who does not approve of their proceedings, and to his aid comes, in a trice a Fairy Queen, who orders the transformations leading to regular comic business; the pantomimic quartette being *Harlequin*, Mr. C. Brown; *Columbine*, Miss Emma Horne; *Pantaloon*, Mr. W. A. Barnes (the Transatlantic pantomimist); and *Clown*, 'the great Flexmore', perhaps in most respects the best *Clown* of the day. Some little delay took place in the setting of Mr. Wm. Beverley's scene 'the Golden Groves of Good Humour', in which these transformations took place (and for which the indulgence of the audience was asked), but when it made its appearance its magnificence amply compensated for any annoyance occasioned by the interruption. The Watteau of scene-painters has seldom produced anything to surpass this one effort: glittering with pale silvery hues, innumerable jewelled pillars supporting the crystal roof, and the whole crowded with nymphs standing on golden pedestals. A burst of loud and protracted applause greeted its production, and secured the triumph of the piece. The comic business opened in 'Adulteration-buildings, Turmeric-row, Red-lion-square', where some telling exposures were made of the tricks of trade, which the publication of Dr. Hassall's analyses has lately rendered so notorious. From these scenes of imposture it is but a step to the region of legitimate imposition—'the Wizard's Laboratory in the Castle of Mephistopheles, Heligoland', where *Clown* and *Pantaloon* display their handicraft in some of the Wizard's most popular tricks, including the Magic Portfolio and the marvellous Extinguisher; then by a sudden transition so sudden as almost to look like an accident—the scene falling down over the performers as they stand on the stage—we find ourselves in a cornfield in view of the new Castle of Balmoral. The subsequent scenes are full of variety and bustle, and appropriate hits at some of the prevailing nuisances of the day:—street musicians, athletes, patent perambulators, Dirty Father Thames, &c.; the whole interspersed with wondrous evolutions by the indefatigable Flexmore, including a burlesque equestrian performance on two wooden horses; and all the multifarious incidents of bewitched doors and windows, haunted coal-holes, magic bottles, self-acting bells, misplaced and misused policemen, &c., which traditionally fill up the measure of a Christmas

132 Going to the pantomime – almost as elaborate and exciting a Christmas ritual as preparing for Christmas itself (1853).

133 Engaging children for the Christmas pantomime at Drury Lane Theatre. Urchins from the neighbourhood gathered at the stage door of the theatre in the hope of being selected for minor parts in the production (1867).

134 Backstage preparations on some of the enormous masks worn in the pantomimes (1870).

135 Rehearsing for the pantomime at the Crystal Palace (1868).

175

HARLEQUIN THE ONE-EYED BLACKSMITH.

Ha! one-ogled blacksmith, what are you about?
Your sight's "all my eye" I have not the least doubt.
But, if you've a spark left of principle too,
You will not keep forging the way that you do!

The Victorian taste for melodrama spilled over into the pantomimes and burlesques that appeared on the stage the moment Christmas was over. Fantastic masks and costumes were worn by the players. Highly complicated scenery was the order of the day, and fairy-tale plots mixed fact and fable at will. 'Harlequin the one-eyed Blacksmith' – what child wouldn't be frightened by this grotesque mask? (**136**), 'King Jamie, or Harlequin and the magic fiddle' (**137**), 'Moon Queen and King Night' – the Baron arrives (**138**), and 'Oliver Cromwell, or Harlequin Charley over the Water and the Maid of Patty's Mill' (**139**).

136

137

138

139

Pantomime. The concluding scene, 'the Apotheosis of ye Belle Aliance', designed by M. Guerin, is a masterpiece of scenic design and structural contrivance. In the midst are mourners at the tomb of the slain; on either side, groups of soldiers, representing every regiment in the English, French, and Sardinian army; and above, the victors, enthroned and crowned with coronals of valour by the Genius of Victory, who descends from the skies to complete the tableau. The highest credit is due to everyone concerned in getting up this splendid pantomime, which we have no doubt will command a long and profitable run. The Wizard received a hearty welcome on his first appearance in his magic arena—an earnest of the high appreciation in which all his efforts to amuse are appreciated by his friends—the public.

Drury Lane.—The title of the pantomime at this house is 'Hey Diddle Diddle; or Harlequin King Nonsense and the Seven Ages of Man'. It is a happy idea, well worked out. The mere statement of it in the advertising column is, as it were, a poem—the performance on the stage is a poem acted. The usual formations introduce us to a succession of gorgeous scenes and brilliant tricks. The scenery, painted by Mr. Beverley, is worthy of his reputation. With Boleno for *Clown*, Veroni for *Harlequin*, Tanner for *Pantaloon*, and Mdme Boleno for *Columbine*, the pantomime went off admirably. Duplicates of these characters were also given; but we do not think that they added at all to the effect of the tricks.

Princess.—The performances at this theatre on Wednesday evening consisted of the 'Heir at Law', and the new Christmas pantomime of 'Harlequin and the Maid and the Magpie; or, the Fairy Paradisa and Hanky-Panky the Enchanter'. The house was crowded long before the orchestra had assembled. Greater attention was paid to the admirable acting in Colman's comedy than might have been expected, considering how much the holiday folks must have been occupied with anticipations of the Christmas novelty. The overture to the pantomime consisted of a *pot-pourri* of those popular tunes which the professors of the street-organ have been insisting on during the past year, and was exceedingly well played. The household story of the 'Maid and the Magpie' is already well known. The rôle of *Annette*, the unfortunate maid of Palaiseau, was taken by Mr. Daly, and that of the *Magpie* by Mr. Saker; the good genius of the piece, the *Fairy Paradisa*, Queen of the Island of Birds, being represented by Miss Kate Terry; and the evil genius, *Hanky-Panky*, the Enchanter, by Mr. F. Cooke. *Annette*, having been taken under the special protection of *Paradisa*, *Hanky Panky* conceives the plan of annoying his rival by persecuting her protégée. The scheme of the 'silver spoon' is carried into execution through the instrumentality of the *Magpie*, and *Annette* is carried to prison. The discovery of the missing spoon at the last moment defeats the malicious purposes of the Enchanter and completes the triumph of the Good Fairy. The customary transformation takes place; masks and disguises are thrown aside, and our old friends, *Clown, Harlequin, Pantaloon*, and *Columbine* (personated by Messrs. Huline, Paulo, and Cormack, and Miss C. Adams) commence their gambols. The scenes throughout are of the most gorgeous description, and do great credit to the artists who conceived and executed them. The first scene, the 'Fairy Aviary of Queen Paradisa', in which are discovered the Fairy Queen herself, surrounded by her maids of honour in the shape of resplendent Canaries, her body-guard of the First Royal Goldfinches, and other dignitaries of the feathered tribe, in the shape of Larks, Humming-birds, Tom-tits, Sparrows, &c., presents a *coup-d'œil* of unparalleled magnificence: The transformation scene, consisting of the 'Golden Bowers of Groundsell and the Silver Avenues of Chickweed', completes the wonders of the first portion of the entertainment. The Harlequinade is in every respect equal to that of 'Blue-Beard', produced at this theatre last Christmas. More praise than this it would be impossible to give. Miss Caroline Adams (engaged at the last moment as a substitute for Miss Phœbe Beale, who unfortunately sprained her ankle at the rehearsal) danced with extreme grace and elegance; while Messrs. Huline, Cormack, and Paulo sustained the high character they have obtained as pantomimists. But, perhaps, the most interesting feature of the whole entertainment was the introduction of Mr. Tanner and his *troupe* of dogs, whose performances are justly styled 'wonderful'. Had we space, we might give an account of their extraordinary feats. But for fear of being charged with exaggeration, all we shall say is, 'Go and see them'. The last scene but one consisted of a 'Juvenile Version of "King Henry the Eighth"', the whole of the characters being performed by children. The pantomime concluded with a 'general reconciliation and union of all parties', and the curtain fell on a splendid spectacle—the Fairy Temple in the realms of Paradisa—amidst a *furore* of applause.

Between the ending of the Christmas holiday and the return to school, Victorian children could still look forward to the parties—a thrilling ride through the snow to a friend's house, the games, the dancing, the charades and perhaps even a conjuror or Punch and Judy. And at the end of it all, a present for everyone and the journey home. A Victorian writer who sensibly hid his identity under the letters M. L. wrote enthusiastically, if a little archly, about children's parties in 1855, imputing their existence, like that of the Christmas tree, to the German influence:

Of late years a pleasant custom has grown up in England—introduced, if I mistake not, with the Christmas-tree from Germany. I mean the practice of giving children's parties—not hobbledehoy balls, where some are too old to be childish, and not old enough to be manly or womanly, as the case may be—but downright children's parties, where after the first ten minutes Formality calls her coach and retires for the evening. As a *paterfamilias*, I contrive now and then to gain admission to some of those delightful gatherings, and, sitting down quietly in a corner, participate in the enjoyment of the scene, without disturbing it. In such assemblages there are smiling faces worth looking at, for the sunshine upon those dimpled cheeks and rosy lips and in those sparkling eyes is real and honest, and not the sham that too often hides aching hearts and envious thoughts, or blighted hopes. You never doubt the truthfulness of the mirth which makes the welkin ring, nor question the existence of the innocent jollity whose exuberance escapes from the twinkling feet of the happy dancers. We are sure that it cannot always be so, that change will come, and it would be a sorry sight indeed to look upon a gathering of the same beings when twenty years have passed, and to know and see all that time has done. Enough for the present to be certain that the little revellers we are now observing are innocent and happy, and to feel assured that those joyous eyes have never wept a tear which flowed from the heart, but that their 'hottest drops' have been shed over the fractured nose of a wax doll, and to be comforted by the thought that those curly-headed gallants dividing plum-cake with blondes and brunettes are quite as unconscious of their powers of fascination as they will be thirty years hence, when their curly pates are bald, and their little noses are crowned with spectacles.

... There were no Christmas trees when you and I, Mr Fifty, were boys; but do you not remember many a joyous game of snapdragon, hunt-the-slipper, and hot cockles, that even now make some of your wrinkles look like smiles? Take my advice, Fifty; give a children's party, and make sure of passing one happy night this merry Christmas time.

History does not relate whether 'Mr Fifty' ever did give a children's party. But if not he might well have passed one happy night at a grown-up dance. For the Victorians Christmas was the season for all kinds of parties—Grand Balls, Fancy-Dress Balls, Hunt Balls, and, for the larger households, staff dances. Contemporary illustrations make some of these adult parties look fairly stultifying and perhaps, after all, 'Mr Fifty' would have been more at home at the dance at Fezziwig's warehouse, which Charles Dickens described with such obvious relish in *A Christmas Carol*:

'Hilli-ho!' cried old Fezziwig, skipping down from the high desk with wonderful agility. 'Clear away, my lads, and let's have lots of room here! Hilli-ho, Dick! Cheer up, Ebenezer!'

140 Some of the fantastic scenic constructions in Victorian pantomimes.

141 A Victorian family enjoys a pantomime – the youngest finds it rather frightening (*c.* 1870).

Clear away! There was nothing they wouldn't have cleared away, or couldn't have cleared away, with old Fezziwig looking on. It was done in a minute. Every movable was packed off, as if it were dismissed from public life forevermore; the floor was swept and watered, the lamps were trimmed, fuel was heaped upon the fire; and the warehouse was as snug, and warm, and dry, and bright a ball-room as you would desire to see upon a winter's night.

In came a fiddler with a music-book, and went up to the lofty desk and made an orchestra of it and tuned like fifty stomach-aches. In came Mrs. Fezziwig, one vast, substantial smile. In came the three Misses Fezziwig, beaming and lovable. In came the six followers whose hearts they broke. In came all the young men and women employed in the business. In came the housemaid with her cousin the baker. In came the cook with her brother's particular friend the milkman. In came the boy from over the way, who was suspected of not having board enough from his master, trying to hide himself behind the girl from next door but one who was proved to have had her ears pulled by her mistress; in they all came, anyhow and everyhow. Away they all went, twenty couple at once; hands half round and back again the other way; down the middle and up again; round and round in various stages of affectionate group-

142 'The schoolboy's notion of what a Christmas pantomime *ought* to be (1867).

143 Costumes for a Christmas fancy-dress ball. 'Buttons in Elizabethan garb was not altogether a success!' (1882).

144 Fancy dress costumes at Our Boys' Clothing Company—a Little Boy Blue suit, a pierrot Costume and a New South Wales Lancer, to name but three.

145 'Original Fancy Costumes' for the ladies.

146 A horse and trap takes a Victorian family through the snow to a Christmas party (1859).

147 'The dance, like most dances after supper, was a merry one, (*c.* 1890).

148 Staff and gentry mix at the Christmas dance – supposedly on equal footing (1891).

149 The first quadrille (1873).

150 The last galop (1873).

151 One of the most popular games at a children's party—make-believe. Here, in 'The Tournament', the Princess presides from her throne (1865).

152 Punch and Judy show at a Christmas party (*c.* 1850).

153 'A present for everyone'—the children draw lots from the top hat for prizes on
the Christmas tree (1858).

154 Twelfth Night – 'the last night of the mistletoe' (1859).

ing, old top couple always turning up in the wrong place; new top couple starting off again, as soon as they got there; all top couples at last, and not a bottom one to help them.

When this result was brought about the fiddler struck up 'Sir Roger de Coverley'. Then old Fezziwig stood out to dance with Mrs. Fezziwig. Top couple, too, with a good stiff piece of work cut out for them; three or four and twenty pairs of partners; people who were not to be trifled with; people who would dance and had no notion of walking.

But if they had been thrice as many—Oh, four times as many—old Fezziwig would have been a match for them, and so would Mrs. Fezziwig. As to her, she was worthy to be his partner in every sense of the term. If that's not high praise, tell me higher and I'll use it. A positive light appeared to issue from Fezziwig's calves. They shone in every part of the dance like moons. You couldn't have predicted at any given time what would become of them next. And when old Fezziwig and Mrs. Fezziwig had gone all through the dance; advance and retire; both hands to your partner, bow and courtesy, corkscrew, thread the needle, and back again to your place; Fezziwig 'cut'—cut so deftly that he appeared to wink with his legs, and came upon his feet again without a stagger.

When the clock struck eleven the domestic ball broke up. Mr. and Mrs. Fezziwig took their stations, one on either side of the door, and shaking hands with every person individually, as he or she went out, wished him or her a MERRY CHRISTMAS!

Epilogue.

---◆---

Who is it stands on the polished stair,
A merry, laughing, winsome maid,
From the Christmas rose in her golden hair
To the high-heeled slippers of spangled suede
A glance, half daring and half afraid,
Gleams from her roguish eyes downcast;
Already the vision begins to fade—
'Tis only a ghost of Christmas Past.

A Ballad of Old Loves CAROLYN WELLS

---◆---

AND SO with the last dance of the last ball of the season, the Victorian Christmas came to an end. The greenery was taken down on Twelfth Night and the decorations were put away. The children went back to school and the New Year came in. But what memories of that glorious holiday remained to warm cold January dreams! Soon it would be time to start saving and planning, cooking and collecting, writing and wrapping all over again. For the moment, it was a case, sadly, of 'Another Christmas Gone':

The frost white hill still glistens,
Beneath the moonlit skies;
As on the night of Christmas,
Untrod it sleeping lies.
A new born year is waiting,
To meet the early dawn;
And whisper this to all the world,
Another Christmas gone.

The holly berry changes
Its coat of emerald red;
And wreaths we twin'd but lately,
Hang, all their verdure dead;

And round our lonely dwelling
A loneliness is cast;
Our holiday is over,
And Christmas Day is past.

But still our hearts look forward
To many happy years,
Unconscious of our future
Its passing joys and tears:
Our friends around may sooner
Be laid within the clay,
Some present never live to see
Another Christmas Day.

191